Salvation Outside the Church?

Rev. Peter M.J. Stravinskas

Our Sunday Visitor Publishing Division
Our Sunday Visitor, Inc.
Huntington, Indiana 46750

To the Rev. Msgr. Joseph C. Shenrock, P.A.,
as he prepares to celebrate his Golden Jubilee
in Christ's Priesthood,
with gratitude for sending me off to the seminary,
for etching into my consciousness the Lord's intense desire
for the unity of His Church,
and for his priestly friendship and support
for more than three decades.

The Scripture citations used in this work are taken from the *Catholic Edition of the Revised Standard Version of the Bible* (RSV), copyright © 1965 and 1966 by the Division of Christian Education of the National Council of the Churches of Christ in the United States of America. Used by permission. All rights reserved.

Excerpts from the English translation of the *Catechism of the Catholic Church*, second edition, for use in the United States of America, copyright © 1994 and 1997, United States Catholic Conference—Libreria Editrice Vaticana. Used by permission. All rights reserved.

Excerpts from *Vatican Council II: Volume I, Revised Edition: The Conciliar and Post Conciliar Documents* edited by Austin Flannery, O.P., copyright © 1998, Costello Publishing Company, Inc., Northport, N.Y., are used by permission of the publisher, all rights reserved.

English translation of *Dominus Iesus* (with minor modifications including American-style punctuation and spelling) from the Vatican website, *www.vatican.va*.

Every reasonable effort has been made to determine copyright holders of excerpted materials and to secure permissions as needed. If any copyrighted materials have been inadvertently used without proper credit being given in one form or another, please notify Our Sunday Visitor in writing so that future editions may be corrected accordingly.

Copyright © 2002 by Our Sunday Visitor Publishing Division, Our Sunday Visitor, Inc.

With the exception of short excerpts for critical review, no part of this book may be reproduced or transmitted in any form or by any means, electronic or mechanical, including photocopying, recording, or by any information storage or retrieval system, without permission in writing from the publisher: Write:

Our Sunday Visitor Publishing Division
Our Sunday Visitor, Inc.
200 Noll Plaza
Huntington, IN 46750

ISBN: 1-931709-36-X (Inventory No. T23)
LCCN: 2002107136

Cover design by Rebecca Heaston
Cover photo by Gregorio Borgia, courtesy AP/Wide World Photos; used with permission

Interior design by Sherri L. Hoffman

PRINTED IN THE UNITED STATES OF AMERICA

Contents

⸙

Preface

A CURSORY REVIEW OF MY CHILDHOOD and adolescence would seem to make me an unlikely candidate to write a book on ecumenical and interreligious affairs. Or maybe not, under closer scrutiny and analysis.

For all practical purposes, I grew up in a "Catholic ghetto" of the 1950s and '60s. Sixteen of the seventeen families in our apartment house in Newark were Catholic, with the other an Anglican.[1] Even non-Catholics identified their neighborhood by the name of the parish. I did not have a non-Catholic friend until seventh grade. Father Leonard Feeney was censured by the Holy See for his adamant adherence to an extreme interpretation of "*Extra Ecclesiam, nulla salus*" ("Outside the Church, no salvation"); I think my father secretly supported Feeney. All that said, I cannot recall a single time when the priests and nuns presented Jews and Protestants in a disrespectful manner, albeit noting the theological errors or inadequacies of their teachings. Interestingly enough, although the Second Vatican Council occurred during the middle of my elementary and secondary education, its influence on my attitudes toward non-Catholics was minimal, perhaps because I had never been exposed to any kind of negative stereotypes to start with.

When I was a junior in high school, a young priest — Father Joseph Shenrock — came into my life. Father Shenrock — for whom I ended up working as a seminarian and likewise living with as a priest — became the founding director of the ecumenical commission for the Diocese of Trenton. As a result, I found myself forming interesting contacts, including membership in an ecumenical clergy book-review club at Princeton Theological Seminary, where I met impressive and holy men like Bruce Metzger, James McCord, and Paul Ramsey.

Working in the Diocese of Boise as a young priest, I was appointed vice-chairman of the ecumenical commission and eventually became the first priest elected chairman of the state council of churches. It was also in Boise that I helped launch the local Anglican-Roman Catholic Dialogue, as well as making overtures toward the Mormons, especially for collaboration on "family value" issues.

My work with the Catholic League for Religious and Civil Rights also provided a venue for joint projects and programs with Jews and Evangelicals on matters like freedom of choice in education and the pro-life cause, as well as forging a formidable coalition to combat secularization and bigotry at one and the same time. And how can I omit the inestimable experience of teaching Catholic theology in the Graduate School of Drew University (an institution with roots in Methodism), but especially the wonderful relationship with the dean, the Rev. James Pain, who exemplifies Christian gentlemanliness?

Now, the reader is undoubtedly asking, "How does a kid from a Catholic ghetto become an 'ecumaniac'? Especially one with such a reputation for adherence to the Catholic 'party line' in all ways and for his leadership in Catholic apologetics? And one who has brought so many converts into the Church?"

Deeper reflection would suggest that coming from a strong Catholic culture, and with strong catechesis under one's belt, actually prepares one for ecumenical and interreligious dialogue. Indeed, confidence breeds openness. Years ago, the National Opinion Research Center in Chicago noted that Catholics who had attended Catholic schools for ten years or more were exponentially more willing to enter into such dialogue than Catholics who had not had the benefit of Catholic schooling, who often tended to be very defensive in their dealings with non-Catholics, largely due to a long-standing need to protect themselves and their faith from external attacks.

Similarly, there is no contradiction between holding the necessity of the Church for salvation, with a concomitant commitment to evangelization, and a deep respect for those outside the visible boundaries of the Catholic Church. One finds the primary models of this approach within the documents of the Second Vatican Council and in the entire pontificate of Pope John Paul II; in truth, orthodox theology, mission-mindedness, and theological openness must be kept in a healthy, creative tension, which has been the aim of the present work.

This volume is a kind of anthology of my thinking on these matters over a long period of time. Some are very tightly reasoned theological treatises, often enough delivered as lectures at theological conferences; others are more popularized texts, seeking to summarize various ecclesiastical documents. It seems to me that this would be an ideal text for a seminary course or in a parish RCIA program; it would also be of value to any informed Catholic (clerical, Religious, or lay) who is interested in the unity of the Church and in thinking of creative (and faithful) ways of participating in the movement toward Christian unity.

If the reader comes away with any thoughts on this important topic for the Church and the world of the third millennium, I hope it would come down to being equally committed to three: the unicity of Jesus Christ; the uniqueness of the Catholic Church as the sacrament of salvation; and the importance of rejoicing in the truth wherever it is found and in whatever degree it is found.

These convictions are not new to the Church; they are found in the witness of the New Testament itself. They are rediscovered convictions that the Holy Spirit has awakened in the Church in these days, causing us to pray, with St. Paul, that the God Who "began a good work in [us] will bring it to completion at the day of Jesus Christ" (Phil 1:6).

The "new" St. Peter's Basilica was completed in the midst of the Protestant Reformation. Bernini constructed his magnificent colonnade as a symbol, he said, of Mother Church's loving and warm embrace of the entire human family, keeping within Catholic unity those who never strayed and ready to welcome back those who had. Thus, it is an apt image to grace the cover of this book, whose theme is the Church as the source and instrument of eternal salvation for the whole human race.

St. Paul, the Apostle to the Gentiles, was not lacking in an appreciation for the mysterious workings of grace, in all people, leading him to rhapsodize thus:

> For this reason I bow my knees before the Father, from whom *every* family in heaven and on earth is named, that according to the riches of his glory he may grant you to be strengthened with might through his Spirit in the inner man, and that Christ may dwell in your hearts through faith; that you, being rooted and grounded in love, may have power to comprehend with all the saints what is the breadth and length and height and depth, and to know the love of Christ which surpasses knowledge, that you may be filled with all the fulness of God.

May his concluding flourish be echoed by us:

> Now to him who by the power at work within us is able to do far more abundantly than all that we ask or think, to him be glory *in the Church and in Christ Jesus* to all generations, for ever and ever. Amen [Eph 3:14-21; emphasis added].

CHAPTER ONE

~~~

The Necessity of the Church

Excerpted and adapted from "The Necessity of the Church," an address for the Catholic Apologetics Series for the Third Millennium of the Archdiocese of Portland in Oregon, on April 25, 1998.

Introduction

SLOGANS CAN BE DANGEROUS. For example, "Remember the Alamo!" rings out with calls for vindictive revenge. "The immemorial Tridentine Mass" suggests that other forms of the Eucharistic Sacrifice just don't "cut it" historically, doctrinally, or liturgically. "The active participation of the faithful" has been used to justify frenetic activity and odd forms of lay involvement in the action of the Sacred Liturgy. "We are Church" is a mischievous expression often uttered to give credibility to dissent from the authentic doctrine of the divinely ordained teachers of the Church's hierarchy by an appeal to American principles of political equality.

The truth of the matter is that slogans can be useful, so long as we know that they generally conceal as much of the truth as they reveal. In other words, like all shorthand expressions, slogans have value as far as they go and as long as those using them realize their limitations.

And so it is with the slogan that occupies our attention today: "*Extra Ecclesiam, nulla salus*" ("Outside the Church, no salvation"). It will be our task today to examine this theological slogan from the perspectives of history and theology, and then to make some applications for contemporary Church life, especially as that influences such critical spheres as ecumenism and evangelization. I should note at the outset my indebtedness to Jesuit Father Francis A. Sullivan, for his magisterial study on this topic in *Salvation Outside the Church? Tracing the History of the Catholic Response*;[2] I enthusiastically recommend this work of Father Sullivan's to any who desire a more in-depth analysis than what I can provide in this necessarily brief overview.

Some folks in the audience today are old enough to remember another Jesuit priest by the name of Leonard Feeney; others of us have heard of him from our parents or from books. In abbreviated form, permit me to offer the broad outlines of what made the man famous — or infamous.

Father Feeney was a brilliant and popular chaplain at Harvard University; young men such as Bernard Law and Avery Dulles were deeply influenced by him. They are now, as you probably know, respectively, the Archbishop of Boston and one of the finest convert-theologians the Church has known since Cardinal Newman. At any rate, Father Feeney began to preach and teach a form of *"extra Ecclesiam"* which the then-Archbishop of Boston, Richard Cushing, found problematic. When asked either to modify his position or to be silent, Father Feeney responded by accusing the Archbishop himself of heresy, leading to an investigation of Feeney's work by the Holy See, with the attendant decision by the Jesuit Order to silence him. When he refused to accept this decision, he was dismissed from the Society of Jesus and eventually excommunicated (with the approval of Pope Pius XII) in 1953, taking with him many men and women whom he formed into a community of Religious and laity — all committed to his extreme interpretation of *"extra Ecclesiam."*

Nineteen years later, during the pontificate of Paul VI, Father Feeney was reconciled with the Church, bringing back into Catholic unity many (but not all) of his disciples. I am told that now-Cardinals Law and Dulles were active participants in that reconciliation process, which occurred but a few years before the death of the old man.

Now, many have pointed with irony to the fact that the priest himself who had preached a rigid understanding of the doctrine of no salvation outside the Church nearly died outside the Church! Of course, Father Feeney surely did not consider himself outside the Church and undoubtedly deemed his detractors (whether the Father

General of the Jesuits or the Archbishop of Boston or even the Sovereign Pontiff himself) to be heretics who themselves were, on that count, outside the Church. One interesting but perhaps not surprising footnote to this entire saga is the epitaph on Father Feeney's tomb, an epitaph which many assert was not his personal choice. Can anyone guess what it says? "*Extra Ecclesiam, nulla salus*"! And to think that the scholarly and sensitive Jesuit could have just as easily been remembered for one of his many poems that we learned in grammar school, "Lovely Lady Dressed in Blue."

Well, let us leave Father Feeney to the judgment of history and, even more importantly, to the judgment of Almighty God. So, let us see where Father Feeney got his slogan and what it has meant to different people at different times in the history of theology.

The first decisive time we meet up with this line is in a profession of faith drawn up by Pope Innocent III in 1208: "We believe in our hearts and confess with our lips that there is one Church, not that of the heretics, but the holy Roman Catholic and apostolic Church, outside of which we believe that no one is saved."[3] Reacting to the Albigensian heretics in 1215, the Fathers of the Fourth Lateran Council (still during the reign of Innocent III) employed a formula that perfectly echoed the earlier one: "There is one universal Church of the faithful, outside of which no one at all is saved."[4] A papal bull of Boniface VIII, *Unam Sanctam*, asserted: "We are obliged by our faith to believe and to hold that there is one holy catholic and apostolic Church; indeed, we firmly believe and sincerely confess this, and that outside this Church, there is neither salvation nor the remission of sins."[5] In fact, Boniface put an even finer point on it all by adding, "Moreover, we declare, state, and define that for every human creature, it is a matter of strict necessity for salvation to be subject to the Roman Pontiff."[6] And the beat goes on through successive statements of the Magisterium for centuries, as even a cursory glance through Denzinger-Schönmetzer's enchiridion of Catholic doctrine would demonstrate.[7] That list, it should be recognized, would include even the Second Vatican Council.[8]

The expression that occupies today, however, did not emerge full-grown from the brow of Zeus in 1208. Indeed, its substance, if not its precise formulation, had a most ancient pedigree, to which we should presently turn our attention.

A Historical Overview of the Doctrine

After the infant Church made her preaching debut on the first Christian Pentecost and St. Peter found himself in prison, he gives voice to our doctrine when he says before the Sanhedrin: "And there is salvation in no one else [that is, Jesus Christ], for there is no other name under heaven given among men by which we must be saved" (Acts 4:12). Very soon, however, Christians began to ask some questions, based on another scriptural insight gleaned from the First Epistle of St. Paul to Timothy, where we read that Almighty God "desires all men to be saved and to come to the knowledge of the truth" (2:4). The teaching contained in this second biblical citation we have come to call "the universal salvific will of God." So, those first Christians wondered, how does one reconcile the unique and absolute nature of God's self-revelation in Christ with the Father's will to save all men — along with the realization that perhaps millions of people (both Jews and Gentiles) had been born and died before the Father had sent His Son into our world?

The first Christian thinker to tackle this thorny problem was St. Justin Martyr in the second century. In his apologetical work, *Dialogue with Trypho the Jew*, he explained that Jews who lived before Christ would nonetheless experience salvation if they had done "those things which are universally, naturally, and eternally good" (that is, "pleasing to God"), so that "they shall be saved in the resurrection, together with their righteous forefathers, Noe, Henoch, Jacob, and others, together with those who believe in Christ, the Son of God" (n. 45).

We should not miss that, by speaking of people performing deeds that are "universally, naturally, and eternally good," this apologist likewise opened up the door of salvation for Gentiles who had lived before Christ's coming, in observance of the natural law. Rather boldly, he declares: "Whereas those [Gentiles] who lived then, or who live now, according to reason are Christians. Such as these can be confident and unafraid."[9]

But now, another question surfaces: What about people who had lived during the Christian era but were not members of the Church? Given the time constraints under which we are operating, I shall be able to do little more than offer you representative responses.

St. Ignatius of Antioch condemned both "a maker of schism" and anyone who follows such as being ineligible to "inherit the Kingdom of God."[10]

Clearly, a personal decision and thus personal guilt are involved in both instances. St. Cyprian — the Bishop of Carthage in North Africa, who was martyred in 258 — addressed himself to the Gnostics and warned them that their disobedience to legitimate ecclesiastical authority put them outside the Church, and that "there can be no salvation for anyone except in the Church."[11] In a later letter, he makes the case even more forcefully: ". . . there is no salvation outside the Church."[12] In his treatise "On the Unity of the Church," Cyprian gives us the classic line: "You cannot have God for your Father if you have not the Church for your mother" (n. 6).

This Church Father was what today we would call a "hard-liner," denying validity to any sacrament administered by any heretic or schismatic. Ultimately, the Church — under the influence of the argumentation of St. Augustine — judged Cyprian too rigoristic. At the same time, however, we must observe that Cyprian addressed himself only to heretics and schismatics, and not to the broader question of those who had never become Christians.

A new moment arrived in Christian history when the Roman persecutions not only ceased but Christianity found itself declared the religion of the empire. What had also changed was the presumption that some people could be held blameless of not accepting the Gospel only because it had never been preached to them. And so, we discover Fathers like St. Ambrose of Milan grounding his negative judgment on their salvation in the fact that "the faith has been spread to all peoples."[13] Similarly, an Eastern Father, St. Gregory of Nyssa, argued that since "the call has gone out to all,"[14] how could we deem some to be invincibly ignorant of the Gospel message? St. John Chrysostom used the very same logic.[15]

Nevertheless, we must stress that even in this new situation all our authors were careful to walk the theological tightrope in such a fashion as to hold fast simultaneously to the fundamental teaching regarding God's universal salvific will. In other words, given the assumption that Jews and Gentiles alike had now had ample opportunity to hear the proclamation of the Gospel, their refusal to enter the Church could only be judged as obstinacy or hardness of heart. In short, it was their fault and no one else's, especially not God's.

St. Augustine came onto the theological scene with assessments that can be summarized thus:

- Salvation for both Jews and Gentiles who lived before the coming of Christ, provided they had some kind of implicit faith in Him (how this could occur, Augustine does not explain).
- No salvation for Christian heretics or schismatics.
- No salvation for Jews or pagans living since the beginning of the Christian era.
- No salvation for any unbelievers, even those who never heard the Gospel preached.

On this last point, one of Augustine's followers, St. Prosper of Aquitaine, distanced himself from his master. Prosper appears to have known of some distant lands where the light of the Gospel had not yet reached, making him conclude that "we have no doubt that in God's hidden judgment, for them also a time of calling has been appointed, when they will hear and accept the Gospel which now remains unknown to them."[16]

In spite of Augustine's greatness, several of his opinions never gained acceptability in the Church. Among them, we can list the following theories:

- That God would condemn unbaptized infants to hell, simply because of the inheritance of original sin.

- That God would justly condemn adults who had never had the chance to be presented with the Gospel — again, due solely to original sin's hold on them.
- That some people would suffer eternal damnation for no other reason than God's lack of interest in saving them!

As we reflect on these Augustinian positions, this might be the occasion to underscore the fact that just because someone is a saint or even a Doctor of the Church does not make his entire body of teaching acceptable; only the Church's Magisterium can decide on what is and is not consonant with her understanding of the truth of Christ. Interestingly enough, while Cyprian got the doctrine of "*extra Ecclesiam*" right and Augustine got some other points wrong, it was Augustine who corrected Cyprian's more extreme positions rejecting the validity of the sacraments of heretics and schismatics.

The next major figure to consider in our very hasty historical overview is St. Thomas Aquinas. As one might expect, the Angelic Doctor made many distinctions and offered many nuances to the received tradition. In summary form, we find the following points:

1. On the specific issue of "no salvation outside the Church," Aquinas held that this is the case because it is only in the Church that one is offered both faith and the sacraments, which bring us salvation.
2. Regarding faith in Christ, Aquinas taught that implicit faith — not necessarily explicit — was necessary, surely before the Lord's coming but even (he would say) for some time after His coming.
3. Since the advent of Christ, St. Thomas believed that faith in Christ had to be explicit — even for those to whom the Gospel was never preached. How could that happen? He thought that God would provide such individuals with some type of extraordinary revelation, thus giving them the opportunity to respond or not.

4. On the universality of God's salvific will, he was one with most medievals in believing that God would offer the needed grace to anyone who did not place an obstacle in the way; the standard theological axiom said, "To one who does what lies in his power, God does not deny grace."

5. Aquinas's evaluation of unbelief (in the sense of a refusal to believe in Christ) in his own day, whether for Jews or Muslims, was simple: They were guilty of sin. He allowed that ignorance diminished culpability, but he maintained that such ignorance would be hard to verify for either the Jews or the Muslims of his time.

6. While Aquinas stressed the necessity of Baptism for entrance into eternal life, he also envisioned some people, unable to be baptized, who nonetheless had a desire either to be baptized or at least to be saved and were essentially willing to do whatever God wanted them to do, in order to be saved. The reason he gave for what we have come to term "baptism of desire" is quite instructive. He said that such a one "can obtain salvation without being actually baptized, on account of the person's desire for baptism, which desire is the outcome of faith that works through charity, whereby God, Whose power is not tied to visible sacraments, sanctifies a person inwardly."[17] This insight must be deeply appreciated: God is not bound to the sacraments. What does Aquinas mean? That the Lord Who established the Church and instituted the sacraments as the ordinary means of salvation remains, however, always sovereign in His judgments and actions. He Who made sacraments is likewise free to bestow His grace in other ways.

7. St. Thomas raised the possibility of whether someone can commit a venial sin while still in the state of original sin. In the context of that discussion, he made the somewhat amazing statement that if a person "orders himself toward the proper end, through grace he will receive the remission of original sin."[18] Again, we see a willingness to posit a kind of "baptism of desire."

It is against this backdrop of Thomistic teaching that we can look at further developments within the community of theologians and in the Magisterium. Two major theological facts need to be considered next: a papal decree and a conciliar decree.

Pope Boniface VIII in 1302, facing fierce political opposition, found it necessary to state, in the strongest of terms, the supremacy of the papacy over temporal rulers. It is in this light that we must interpret his famous *Unam Sanctam*. Therein, we read the following: "Moreover, we declare, state and define that for every human creature it is a matter of necessity for salvation to be subject to the Roman Pontiff."[19] It needs to be noted that this line from Boniface's bull is but a direct quotation from Aquinas's *Contra Errores Graecorum*, wherein he is simply equating subjection to the Pope with membership in the Church of Christ.[20]

The second historical document we should confront is from the Council of Florence in 1431, which was convoked to heal the rift between the Churches of East and West. The Decree for the Jacobites (another name for the Coptics) contains the following article: "[The holy Roman Church] . . . firmly believes, professes, and preaches that no one outside the Catholic Church, neither pagans, nor Jews, nor heretics, nor schismatics, can become partakers of eternal life. . . . And no one can be saved, no matter how much he has given in alms, even if he sheds his blood for the name of Christ, unless he remains in the bosom and unity of the Catholic Church."[21]

A careful reading of the text reveals that what the Council Fathers obviously had in mind was not an outright condemnation of those invincibly ignorant of the Gospel message but of those who were obdurate in their rejection of it. It is equally certain that it never would have dawned upon a medieval Christian to suppose that the way Jews and Muslims were often approached with the Gospel (all too often under political and physical duress) did little to convince them that this was a program of life worth considering, let alone that it could truly come from a God of peace and justice. At any rate, the conventional wisdom of that era presumed that the Christian message was indeed sufficiently known that refusal to accept it constituted the sin of unbelief, deemed worthy of eternal damnation.

Theology never develops in a vacuum, and that is clearly the case with the doctrine of "*extra Ecclesiam.*" Onto the scene of theological surety just described came the discoveries of "new worlds" during the fifteenth and sixteenth centuries, causing a "sea change" in thinking as old certainties flew out the window once people realized that there yet remained millions of human beings who had never heard the name of Jesus Christ. What was one to make of them and their eternal salvation, let alone that of their forebears?

Without belaboring it all, a few references to theologians' reactions would be worthwhile. The Dominican Francisco de Vitoria rooted his evaluation in the categories that had been offered earlier by Aquinas. And so, we read: "As St. Thomas says, however, if they [pagans in these newly discovered lands] do what in them lies, accompanied by a good life according to the law of nature, it is consistent with God's providence that He will illuminate them regarding the name of Christ."[22] Vitoria went even further to suggest that if the native peoples were not converting of their own volition, one should not be surprised, given the maltreatment they received all too often at the hands of the conquistadors, who were perceived, frankly, as the hands, the heart, and the voice of Christ by the would-be converts.

A second Dominican, Melchior Cano, dealt with the question by teaching that while a person could attain the remission of original sin by a just life without an explicit faith in Jesus Christ, that would not do for salvation. Here, he held out for some experience before death that would bring about the illumination necessary to make an explicit act of faith in Christ as Redeemer and thus merit the beatific vision.

Yet a third Dominican, Domingo Soto, rejected his confrère's solution as artificial. He returned to St. Thomas's position regarding the salvation of pagans before Christ's coming as being normative for such peoples who lived in his day before being presented with the Gospel.

Albert Pigge, writing in the middle of the sixteenth century, saw issues with a clarity that neither Boniface VIII nor the Fathers of Florence could have seen, for the simple reason that the exploration of the new lands had not yet occurred. Pigge recognized the new situation: "If you say that by now the Gospel of Christ has been sufficiently promulgated in the whole world, so that ignorance can no longer excuse anyone — reality itself refutes you, because every day now numberless nations are being discovered among whom, or among their forefathers, no trace is found of the Gospel ever having been preached. . . ."[23]

With great insight and sensitivity, he goes on to make a specific example of the followers of Islam: "I grant that the Moslems have heard the name of Christians. But they have been so educated that they think that our faith is false and mistaken, while the faith in which they have been educated is the true faith. . . . They do not know anything about divine revelation; they have not seen signs or miracles that would prove their religion false, nor have they heard of them in such a way that they would be truly obliged to believe those who told them of such things." All of this led him to this conclusion: "Therefore, erroneous faith does not condemn, provided the error has a reasonable excuse and that they are invincibly ignorant of the true faith."[24]

The Jansenists in the sixteenth and seventeenth centuries were rigorists in many ways, as everyone knows, but especially in that area of theology that concerns us here. A spiritual forefather of them was the Belgian Michael DeBay; among many of his propositions condemned by Pope St. Pius V in 1567 are the following: "All the works of infidels are sins, and the virtues of the [pagan] philosophers are vices"[25] and the "purely negative infidelity of those to whom Christ has not been preached is a sin."[26]

Over a century later, during the reign of Pope Alexander VIII, the Holy Office condemned theological positions with strong echoes of DeBay. For example, "pagans, Jews, heretics and others of that kind receive no influence at all from Jesus Christ, hence one rightly concludes that their wills are naked and defenseless, totally lacking sufficient grace"[27] or "an infidel necessarily sins in every work"[28] or "everything that does not proceed from supernatural Christian faith, working through love, is sinful."[29] The Holy See's condemnation of these Jansenist teachings is an indication of a willingness to accord some measure of saving grace to those invincibly ignorant of the Christian message.

Taking our time machine up to the nineteenth century, we find no less a stalwart defender of Catholic orthodoxy than Blessed Pope Pius IX making this most nuanced statement in *Singulari Quadam*: ". . . it is also a perfectly well-known Catholic dogma that no one can be saved outside the Catholic Church, and that those who are contumacious against the authority and the definitions of that same Church, and who are pertinaciously divided from the unity of that Church and from Peter's successor, the Roman Pontiff, to whom the custody of the vineyard has been committed by the Savior, cannot obtain eternal salvation."

The operative words, to be sure, are "contumacious" and "pertinaciously." No surprise, then, that in the very same document we find a clarion expression of the possibility of salvation for those who sojourn outside the Church through no fault of their own. And so, we read: "It is known to Us and to you that those who labor in invincible ignorance concerning our most holy religion and who, assiduously observing the natural law and its precepts which God has inscribed in the hearts of all, and being ready to obey God, live an honest and upright life can, through the working of the divine light and grace, attain eternal life." Simply put, Pius IX obviously took seriously the theological discussions of the previous centuries and encapsulated them in the form you just read.

The ball was now back in the court of the theologians to explain how that might happen. Cardinal Johannes Franzelin, a Jesuit and a contemporary of the Pope, took up the challenge and saw the process working in this way: Since justification occurs only through supernatural faith and, as St. Paul teaches, "faith comes from what is heard" (Rom 10:17), the saving message must be proclaimed — the task of the Church. Furthermore, faith orients a person to the Church;

and even if that person will not be joined to the Church on earth, he is oriented toward the eschatological Church, to which the earthly Church is intimately and indissolubly bound. Beyond that, by virtue of their desire for salvation, those not in communion with the Catholic Church have at least an implicit desire for such membership. In short, anyone who is destined for salvation achieves that goal through the Church and by a relationship with her. This analysis found its way into the first draft of the constitution on the Church proposed at Vatican I; due to the outbreak of the Franco-Prussian War, however, this document was tabled as the Council adjourned, *sine die.*

Between the two Vatican Councils, theologians once more sought to develop the Church's understanding of this doctrine of ours. Some fell back on a distinction formed by St. Robert Bellarmine, between those who partook in the visible structure of the Church as the Church's "body" and those who by their interior dispositions participated in her life of grace and charity as belonging to her "soul." Jesuit Father Émile Mersch began to work out a coherent theology of the Church as "the Mystical Body of Christ." The Dominican Father Yves Congar, however, saw pitfalls in this approach that could appear to separate the Church into two different realities, when we know, of course, that there is only one Church, which has both visible and invisible elements. Congar's synthesis, then, was to argue that "elements" of the one true Church existed outside her visible boundaries. Another theologian who proceeded along Congar's lines was Father Henri de Lubac, although de Lubac seemed to think that his solution was rather different. Interestingly, both men ended up as *periti* (expert witnesses) at Vatican II, and both were eventually named cardinals by Pope John Paul II.

Before Vatican II, though, an important ecclesiological document appeared on the horizon in Pope Pius XII's encyclical *Mystici Corporis* in 1943. Eighty years after Pius IX's encyclical, we find Pius XII making this contribution to the question:

> We urge each and every one of [those outside Catholic unity] to be prompt to follow the interior movements of grace,

and to seek earnestly to rescue themselves from a state in which they cannot be sure of their own salvation. For even though, by a certain unconscious desire and wish, they may be related to the Mystical Body of the Redeemer, they remain deprived of so many and so powerful gifts and helps from heaven, which can be enjoyed only within the Catholic Church [n. 101].

I hope you did not miss critical lines such as "they cannot be sure of their own salvation" or "they remain deprived of so many and so powerful gifts." What was he saying? Well, at a minimum, he was acknowledging that although they cannot be certain of their eternal *salvation*, neither they nor we are certain of their eternal *damnation*. And further, that while they are deprived of "many" gifts leading to salvation, they are not deprived of *all* such gifts.

Six years later, this encyclical formed the basis for the response of the Holy Office to the query of Archbishop Cushing regarding the teaching of Father Feeney. And so, the following statement gives an official interpretation to the teaching of Pius XII: "With these prudent words [cited above], the Pope censures those who exclude from eternal salvation all men who adhere to the Church only with an implicit desire; and he also censures those who falsely maintain that men can be saved equally well in all religions."[30] Judged unacceptable were both a facile condemnation of those outside the Church through no fault of their own and a facile religious indifferentism. We are now situated on the eve of the Second Vatican Council, where nearly nineteen hundred years of theological development become crystallized.

To save time and since the documentation is rather readily available, allow me merely to summarize what the Council Fathers ended up doing. While many earlier ecclesiastical documents spoke of those who "really" belonged to the Church, *Lumen Gentium* prefers to speak of those who are "fully" members or not. In this way, we eliminate an "all-or-nothing" approach. "Fullness" admits of degrees, thus taking cognizance of Pius XII's insight that non-Catholic Christians do not possess "all" the means of grace, while retaining some of them. Not being "fully" incorporated into Christ's Church does, nonetheless, mean that one is somewhat incorporated, which happens when one is baptized; for we know that Baptism incorporates us into Christ and into His Body, the Church. No Christ without the Church; no Church without Christ.

This awareness led the Council Fathers to declare in *Unitatis Redintegratio*:

> The brethren divided from us also carry out many liturgical actions of the Christian religion. In ways that vary according to the condition of each church or community, these liturgical actions most certainly can truly engender a life of grace, and, one must say, can aptly give access to the communion of salvation.

The same Decree on Ecumenism continues:

> It follows that these separated Churches and communities as such, though we believe they suffer from the defects already mentioned, have been by no means deprived of significance and importance in the mystery of salvation. For the Spirit of Christ has not refrained from using them as means of salvation which derive their efficacy from the very fullness of grace and truth entrusted to the Catholic Church [n. 3].

Let us highlight a few points here.

First, don't miss the language of "fullness" and "elements," which makes the critical distinction between the possession by the Catholic Church of all that is needed for salvation, while still allowing for aspects of that fullness to be present elsewhere.

Second, the Council Fathers were very careful to refer to "Churches and communities," to underscore the fact that not all non-Catholic Christian bodies have the same degree of what we might dub "Churchiness." To qualify as a "Church," a body must have apostolic succession, which ensures valid Orders and thus a valid Eucharist; those lacking that reality are called "communities."

Third, unabashedly, the decree makes the Catholic Church the norm, the standard, and the source of whatever is good and holy in other Christian communities. Simply put, to the extent that they have retained the *vestigia Ecclesiae* (that is, the vestiges or traces of the Church), they are more or less participants in the life of grace that exists in all its fullness only in the Catholic Church.

Quite logically, then, that very same Council in *Lumen Gentium* gives this sober assessment:

> Basing itself on scripture and tradition, [this sacred synod] teaches that the Church, a pilgrim now on earth, is necessary for salvation: the one Christ is mediator and the way of salvation; he is present to us in his body which is the Church. He himself explicitly asserted the necessity of faith and baptism, and thereby affirmed at the same time the necessity of the Church which men enter through baptism as through a door.

In shorthand form, we see the ongoing, consistent doctrinal commitment. And then, the follow-up:

> Hence they could not be saved who, knowing that the Catholic Church was founded as necessary by God through Christ, would refuse either to enter it, or to remain in it [n. 14].

So, we are face-to-face with the traditional doctrine, made with the accompanying qualifying remarks about a conscious refusal to join or remain within the one Church of Christ.

On the matter of salvation for non-Christians, Vatican II likewise makes some inroads, but along lines that had been sketched out over a long period of theological development. Thus, *Lumen Gentium* talks about "those who have not yet received the Gospel" as being "related to the People of God in various ways" (n. 16), giving different modes of this relationship for Jews, Muslims, and still other non-believers. The Council Fathers, putting themselves in line with so many patristic authors, actually refer to current religious observances of non-believers as a *praeparatio evangelica* ("preparation for the Gospel"), not unlike the attitude of the Fathers of the Church, who spoke of the *logoi spermatikoi* ("seeds of the Word"), which would prepare men's minds and hearts for the full revelation in and through Jesus Christ.

Finally, the conciliar texts go to great lengths to demonstrate the Church to be the "universal sacrament of salvation" (e.g., *Lumen Gentium*, n. 48). What was intended here? Just that the Church's very existence summons or beckons the entire human race to be one in Christ and in His Church. To be sure, the most significant action the Church performs in that regard is her offering of the Eucharistic Sacrifice, which is both an invitation to Catholic unity and a cause of it. Father Francis Sullivan sums up this long and winding historical trail of a dogma in this way: "The necessity of the Church for the salvation of humanity, which the axiom 'No salvation outside the Church' expressed in so negative and misleading a way, is the same truth that has received positive and profound theological expression in Vatican II's presentation of the Church as the 'universal sacrament of salvation.' "[31]

Some Questions and Applications

Now that the teaching has been staked out, what are we to make of it, in light of contemporary questions and problems? What would the Church have us think about the eternal salvation of pagans, atheists, and agnostics? What about the Jews? What about non-Catholic Christians who were born into their particular faith communities? How about people who have willingly and deliberately moved into apostasy, heresy, or schism — someone like Archbishop Marcel Lefebvre? How about those who have followed or supported him? What about people who assert that one religion is as good as another? How about people who remain juridically connected to the Catholic Church while refusing to accept her teachings in a host of fields, let alone live according to them?

In all these diverse circumstances, I think we have both in the long tradition of this dogma and in the rendering of it into contemporary life by the Fathers of the Second Vatican Council a fruitful response. In each instance, we must ascertain the degree of personal engagement, responsibility, and deliberateness. Regarding the non-baptized, Pope John Paul II has recalled that Baptism "is the ordinary way of conversion and grace." But he goes on: "Other ways are not excluded, for 'the Spirit blows where it wills' (cf. Jn 3:8). The Spirit can accomplish this work of salvation by sanctifying man apart from the sacrament, when its reception is not possible."[32]

As far as the Jews are concerned, St. Paul gave us the answer nearly two thousand years ago when he taught that "the gifts and the call of God are irrevocable" (Rom 11:29); and the assurance that they "will be grafted in, for God has the power to graft them in again" (Rom 11:23). Hence, God will save the Jews, as He promised, when He wants to do so and in the way He chooses.

Individuals who find themselves members of non-Catholic Christian bodies, more as an accident of birth or culture than personal conviction, need to be approached with the truth of the Gospel with respect and charity, giving them the opportunity to come to know the full Gospel found only in the Catholic Church. People who leave Catholic unity, with full knowledge and consent, are indeed in peril of eternal damnation, as we saw so clearly enunciated by the Second Vatican Council. Those who aid and abet apostasy, heresy, or schism cannot separate themselves from the effects of those scars on the Body of Christ. That one religion is as good as another is demonstrably false; that elements of truth and holiness can usually be found in any religion can be logically and historically sustained, but why would anyone be content with "second-best" for oneself or allow others to be so enthused?

People who constitute a kind of "fifth column" within the Catholic Church are dishonest. They need to heed the evaluation made by St. Augustine fifteen centuries ago when he observed: "For in the ineffable foreknowledge of God, many who appear to be without are within, while many who appear to be within are without."[33] God is not fooled by games of mental reservation and/or institutional parasitism.

Some Concluding Remarks

In the briefest form possible, then, we can sum up our entire investigation with the brilliant insight of the Fathers of the Second Vatican Council, in *Ad Gentes Divinitus*: "The Church on earth is by its very nature missionary" (n. 2). That is no slogan — and even Father Feeney would agree with me on that!

CHAPTER TWO

⌒

An Overview of Ecumenical History

MANY COMMENTATORS HAVE SUGGESTED that the fundamental agony Our Lord endured on the night before He died was not the prospect of a painful death but the realization that His Church would be plagued by division; hence, the overriding concern of His High Priestly Prayer offered to His heavenly Father in the context of the Last Supper, encapsulated so powerfully in the heartrending petition: ". . . that they may all be one; even as thou, Father, art in me, and I in thee, that they also may be in us, so that the world may believe that thou hast sent me" (Jn 17:21). Unity, it can be seen, is viewed by Christ as the precondition for successful evangelization; unity, however, is possible only when grounded in the truth, as we also read: "Sanctify them in the truth; thy word is truth . . . that they may become perfectly one, so that the world may know . . ." (Jn 17:19, 23).

Nevertheless, we must shamefacedly admit that heresy, schism, and apostasy are nearly as old as the Church, for right within the Lord's public ministry itself we find those who could not accept His doctrine of the Eucharist (and were thus invited to leave by Him [cf. Jn 6]) and the sad betrayal and departure of Judas. Shortly after the Pentecost event, various sects arose within the Christian community to challenge her unity of doctrine, whether the Judaizers (who were condemned in the Acts of the Apostles and the Epistle to the Galatians) or the Gnostics (who preoccupied the author of the Johannine corpus).

However, there have always been people in the Church concerned to bring the lapsed back into full communion, which is the task of ecumenism. Etymologically, *ecumenism* comes from the Greek word that refers to the whole world (*oikumene*) and thus the unity of the whole Church throughout the world. Technically, ecumenism deals only with relations among Christians, leaving dialogue between

Christians and the non-baptized to interreligious experts. Ecumenism comes in many garbs: *theological* (formal conversations between Christian bodies on disputed points of doctrine), *spiritual* (prayer for unity), and *social* (working together in all ways possible, while not sacrificing doctrinal convictions, to make the City of Man resemble more closely the City of God).

In addition to the early breaks from ecclesial unity already noted, some of the more famous (or infamous) in history should be noted: the schism of the Nestorians after the Council of Chalcedon in 451, as well as that of the Monophysites; the 1054 split between the Churches of the East and West; the so-called Great Western Schism, which centered on multiple contenders for the papal throne and the Avignon captivity of the papacy from 1378 to 1418, ending with the Council of Constance; the Protestant Reformation of the sixteenth century, beginning with Martin Luther and now reflected in what some estimate to be 28,000 Protestant denominations five centuries later; a little-noticed but important split within Russian Orthodoxy in the seventeenth century; the creation of the Utrecht schism in 1713 following the Church's condemnation of Jansenism, and then in Germany and Switzerland after Vatican I's definition of infalli-bility in 1871, giving rise to the "Old Catholic Church"; the estab-lishment of the Polish National Catholic Church in Scranton in 1904, stemming from ethnic conflicts but then taking on doctrinal elements; the Aglipayan schism in the early twentieth century in the Philippines; the 1988 excommunication of Archbishop Marcel Lefebvre and the four men he consecrated as bishops in defiance of a papal injunction to the contrary.

Reunions have also occurred, but not with the same regularity and force as the divisions. Some Armenians returned to Catholic unity between 1198 and 1375, as did some Monophysites after the Council of Florence and some Nestorians in the sixteenth century. The Councils of Lyons (1274) and Florence (1438) made efforts at wholesale reconciliations, but with little concrete success. The plea of Cardinal Bessarion at Florence, however, typifies the Church's attitude toward such concerns:

What excuse can we offer to justify our unwillingness to unite? What answer have we to give to God to justify our divisions with our brethren, when to unite us and to bring back to the one fold He Himself came down from heaven, became incarnate, and was crucified? What excuse can we make to our descendants? Even more so to our contemporaries?

Various partial reconciliations took place from the sixteenth to the twentieth centuries, with the most successful involving the Ukrainians at the Treaty of Brest-Litovsk in 1596 and the Ruthenians at the Treaty of Uzhorod in 1646. It is interesting to note that no similar attempts to repair the splintering among various ecclesial communities within Protestantism have been made (at least in a truly organic fashion) or vis-à-vis the Catholic Church. Most recently, some of the excommunicated "Lefebvrists" in Brazil have been reconciled with the Holy See.

When we approach the concrete dimensions of reconciliation, several modes of reunion suggest themselves and have been applied throughout history: "absorption" of other Churches or ecclesial communities; working toward the unity willed by Christ, in the time and by the means He wishes; accepting a kind of "unity in plurality," by taking one another, as is, foregoing in-depth theological discussion or agreement for the sake of some type of unity; evangelical conversions of all concerned by listening to one another's questions and concerns, responding with openness and love.

From a Catholic perspective, genuine unity must be rooted in truth and may never simply be a superficial "agreement to disagree." While we can countenance this kind of arrangement as we move toward the desired full and true communion willed by Christ, the "half-loaf" can never be the goal and can never be settled for.

Ecumenical activity in the nineteenth century was pretty much a Protestant affair, since the Catholic Church viewed the only acceptable ecumenism to be not conversations but conversions — individual or collective — to the Church of Rome. One Protestant experiment was the founding of the YMCA (1878) and YWCA

(1894), which formed the basis for a different kind of ecumenism — the engagement in social and athletic activities for young Christians without reference to denominational differences. Another interesting influence was that of liberalism, which not only had the strange effect of uniting many Protestants in their drift from doctrine but also of bringing together many others in their desire to maintain a doctrinal stance; a case in point of the latter would be the Fundamentalist movement.

A strong desire to evangelize characterized many Protestants coming out of the Pietist mode, popularized by the Methodist Church. As the multiplicity of denominations arrived on the continents of Africa and Asia, the insight of Christ uttered on the night before He died came into the full light of day — namely, that the unity of His disciples would lead others to faith, while their disunity would be a scandal or stumbling block to the work of evangelization. One commentator records a common observation of those being evangelized by the panoply of Protestant communities:

> You have sent us missionaries, who have taught us to know Jesus Christ, and we thank you. But you have also brought us your distinctions and divisions: some preach Methodism, others Lutheranism, Congregationalism, or Episcopalianism. We ask you to preach the Gospel and to let Jesus Christ Himself create, among our peoples and with the help of the Holy Spirit, the Church that answers His requirements and responds to the Spirit of our race. This will be the Church of Christ . . . freed from all the "isms" from which your teaching of the Gospel among us suffers.[34]

Someone like Søren Kierkegaard in Denmark relativized Lutheranism, in the sense that he did not view it as a norm but as a corrective; in other words, he felt that the only justification for the existence of Lutheranism had been to bring about the necessary reforms in the Catholic Church, and that once that task had been accomplished, sectarianism had to cede to unity.

The Oxford Movement sought to "re-Catholicize" Anglicanism. A critically important vehicle for their endeavor was the *Tracts for the Times,* with men like John Keble, E.B. Pusey, and John Henry Newman leading the way for the so-called Tractarians, with their High Church sensibilities, appreciation for the Fathers of the Church, and desire to look and be as "Catholic" as possible. A classic example of this was Newman's Tract 90, in which he tried to put as Catholic a spin on the Thirty-nine Articles of Religion as he could. The biggest difficulty of the Anglo-Catholic movement was that so many of its devotees ended up leaving Anglicanism for Rome. After Newman's departure, the Oxford Movement took a decidedly Roman tilt liturgically, in addition to presenting Anglicanism as part of the Church Catholic and in continuity with the Church of the Middle Ages and of the Fathers.

In order to accomplish this, they continued to develop the "branch theory" of Christianity (which holds that "the Church Catholic" is composed of three branches — Roman Catholicism, Eastern Orthodoxy, and the Anglican Communion — all having equal claims), a theory which Newman had embarked upon years earlier but had abandoned when he saw it as theologically and historically untenable. The Anglo-Catholics were as decidedly hostile to Lutheranism and Calvinism as they were favorable toward things Roman.

In 1857, the Association for the Promotion of Christian Unity was founded by Frederic George Lee and viewed favorably by Cardinal Wiseman but rather opposed by his successor, Cardinal Manning. An 1864 letter of the Holy Office to Catholic bishops of England condemned what the Holy See deemed the excesses of the APCU, so that Catholic membership dissolved until 1921. Anglicans also looked East but found an ultimately unfavorable hearing from Orthodoxy from a doctrinal point of view. In 1867, the Lambeth Conferences were established, as Anglican synods tried to shore up Anglicanism within itself, devising the "Lambeth Quadrilateral," consisting of an adherence to Scripture, the Creeds, the Sacraments of Baptism and Eucharist, and the "historic episcopate," as the essentials of Anglican theology and polity.

However, one might ask, "Just what is the Anglican 'historic episcopate'?" Honesty compels one to admit that it was never accepted by the Catholic Church and was categorically denied in 1896 by Pope Leo XIII's encyclical *Apostolicae Curae*, and eventually also by Moscow in 1948. Many Anglicans were originally quite interested in the convoking of the First Vatican Council but were disappointed by the infallibility definition.

A handful of Catholics in the eighteenth and nineteenth centuries could be classified as ecumenists; among them, one would count Bossuet (who was committed to theological conversations) and Cardinal de Noailles (who stressed "spiritual" ecumenism). Lord Halifax and the Abbé Portal initiated a dialogue, resulting in an 1895 letter from Leo XIII calling for "reconciliation and peace," rather than the heretofore standard call for "submission" to Roman authority. That positive thrust was generally seen as a momentary "flash in the pan" after the promulgation of *Apostolicae Curae,* declaring Anglican Orders to be "absolutely null and utterly void," following the investigation of the papal theological commission charged with studying the question. Nevertheless, the rest of Catholic Europe had been introduced to ecumenism due to the initiatives of Halifax and Portal.

In the United States, coping mechanisms had been developed between the immigrant Catholic Church and mainstream Protestantism, especially due to attitudes and actions of bishops like John England of Charleston, John Ireland of St. Paul, and James Gibbons of Baltimore. In 1836, practical ecumenism was advanced by Bishop William Clancy when cholera ravaged the Carolinas. The Parliament of Religions, which was convened in Chicago in 1892, was joined in by Catholic bishops.

Spiritual ecumenism found a great champion in the person of St. Vincent Pallotti (1795-1850), in his promotion of the Epiphany Octave as a time of special prayer for Christian unity. In 1908, Spencer Jones and Lewis Thomas Wattson, both Anglican clergymen, suggested an octave of prayer for this intention from January 18 (then the feast of the Chair of St. Peter) to January 25 (the feast of the Conversion of St. Paul); the idea was then picked up by Abbé

Couturier in 1935, at which point it spread throughout the Catholic Church.[35]

Leo XIII proposed the Pentecost novena for the same theme, with an emphasis not on individual conversions but on collective reunion. His rather open letter to the Scottish hierarchy in 1898 served as the basis for the ecumenical endeavors of Benedict XV, Pius XI, and Pius XII. In 1902, Patriarch Joachim II of Constantinople sent a letter to all Orthodox Churches calling for stronger ties among themselves and then outreach to other Christian bodies, but this was met with relative indifference; he followed up with a 1904 letter to the same effect and then a 1920 letter to all Christian bodies, outlining an eleven-point program of action.

In 1910, at the World Missionary Conference of Edinburgh, an appeal was made for study of doctrine, resulting in the birth of the Lausanne Conference and the Faith and Order movement. Thirty years later, the Life and Work movement emphasized common action within the sphere of what some have called "practical Christianity." During all of this ecumenical ferment, the Catholic Church remained somewhat aloof, largely due to the strain brought on by the internal problems from Modernism; however, she was not uninterested, as evidenced by the actions of several popes.

Benedict XV assigned Eastern Catholics to be a bridge to the Orthodox, establishing the Oriental Institute in 1917 for this purpose. Although he issued a negative judgment on Catholic participation in a 1918 ecumenical assembly, in 1919 the Holy Office likewise issued a blanket prohibition, but with a mitigating proviso allowing for explicit permission of the Holy See to be sought and obtained.

Pius XI was quite interested in Christian unity, but especially with the East, leading him to reorganize the Oriental Institute in 1922, to mandate the introduction of courses on Eastern Christianity in all Catholic faculties, and to commission the Benedictines to become conversant in Eastern affairs and to establish Byzantine monasteries. The first such community was founded in Belgium in 1925 at Amay, which then moved in 1929 to Chevetogne (where it still is), devoted to prayer for unity and the study of Orthodoxy. In 1923, Pius XI became a precursor of John Paul II's call for the Church to "breathe with both lungs."

In 1924, the Pope praised Catholic ecumenists. He also encouraged Cardinal Désiré Joseph Mercier and the Malines Conversations, even as he continued to oppose the Faith and Order and Life and Work programs, largely because of what he perceived to be their superficiality, in their failure to get to the root of doctrinal difficulties. In 1928, his encyclical *Mortalium Animos* condemned a prevailing tendency toward "pan-Christianity," seeming to put a damper on ecumenical activities with his critique and summons, even if assuring non-Catholics of a kindly hearing:

> The union of Christians cannot be otherwise realized than by favoring the return of the dissidents to the one and true Church of Christ, which they had formerly the misfortune to abandon. Let them therefore return to the common Father. He will welcome them with all his tenderness.

Such a mindset, however, was not limited to the Catholic side of the aisle, for twenty years later Karl Barth was no less emphatic: "Our only attitude with regard to Catholicism is one of mission, of evangelization!"[36] On balance, however, one would have to conclude that a consistent goal of Pius XI's pontificate had been the fostering of mutual knowledge and love, although advocated with great caution.

The Malines Conversations, alluded to earlier, consisted of five meetings held between 1921 and 1926 to promote Anglican-Catholic dialogue. The impetus for these talks seems to have come from the 1920 Lambeth Appeal, which had indicated some Anglican openness to re-ordination, if that would hasten the day of full organic union. Key players were Cardinal Mercier and Lord Halifax, from the Anglican side. The stated goal of these meetings was solely for purposes of clarification and information — to get rid of obstacles. The program was also different from other ecumenical gatherings in two ways: it was limited to a small group (six members) and just two theological traditions.

Halifax admitted, however, that there was a problem of disunity within the Anglican Communion itself, and that all three Anglican participants had "High Church" associations and thus were not representative of the whole Anglican spectrum. The fourth conversation included the Benedictine monk Lambert Beauduin, founder of the monastery at Chevetogne and author of the controversial book *The Church of England United, not Absorbed.* The fifth conversation occurred just after the deaths of Mercier and Portal, the death knell for the conversations.

The World Council of Churches came into being, holding its first gathering in 1948 at Amsterdam and convoking such meetings at roughly seven-year intervals since then in places as diverse as Evanston, Illinois, and Nairobi, Kenya. To this day, the Catholic Church holds back from general membership because of a concern for the theological positions taken, but especially since Catholic membership could give the impression that the Catholic Church now sees herself as but one of many Christian "denominations." The reason for Catholic aloofness from the World Council of Churches was understood by Dr. Lukas Vischer of the Reformed World Alliance in 1988:

> The Roman Catholic Church and the World Council of Churches are not comparable organisms. On the one hand, we have a Church, on the other, a community of Churches. That is why they could not have joined together without difficulty. The Vatican leaders saw this very clearly. That is why it is unfair to reproach them for their lack of ecumenical commitment.

However, the Catholic Church is a permanent member of the Faith and Order Commission, and both Pope Paul VI and Pope John Paul II have addressed their general assemblies.

The *Una Sancta* movement for prayer and conversation was begun in Austria (later moving to Germany) by Father Max Metzger (who was killed by the Nazis in 1944). In 1937, the Dombes Group was formed, using a Cistercian house near Lyons as a base for fraternal gatherings of Catholic and Protestant clergy, for prayer and conversation (twenty from each community); it was intensely theological and spiritual from the start and is still functioning.

At an intellectual level, Josef Lortz, a German Jesuit, made a significant contribution by reviving Luther studies among Catholics, with his work being hailed for its professionalism and objectivity. In truth, most ecumenism before Vatican II took place in Germany and Holland (both had been ravaged by the Protestant Reformation), since there were practical circumstances to pursue such a program in those religiously divided environments; the Holy See's initial reaction was either unfavorable or guarded, perhaps largely due to the fact that Italy had never experienced the scandal of disunity in a serious way and therefore could not respond adequately.

The major impetus to ecumenical endeavors from within Catholicism began with Pope Pius XII during World War II, as he approved of the formation of *Una Sancta*. He also encouraged interdenominational study in Scripture, patristics, and liturgy. In fact, the New American Bible (1970) was a product of the joint efforts of Catholic-Protestant scholarship for twenty-five years.

In 1943, an official acknowledgment of non-Catholic Christians was made in a non-polemical, charitable way in Pope Pius's famous encyclical *Mystici Corporis*:

> Moreover, We trust that the following exposition of the doctrine of the Mystical Body of Christ will be acceptable and useful to those, also, who are without [outside] the fold of the Church. This confidence is based not only on the fact that their good will toward the Church seems to grow from day to day, but also because, while before their eyes today nation rises against nation, kingdom against kingdom, and discord is sown everywhere together with the seeds of envy and hatred, if they turn their gaze to the Church, if they contem-

plate her divinely given unity — by which all men of every race are united to Christ in the bond of brotherhood — they will be forced to admire this fellowship in charity, and with the guidance and assistance of divine grace will long to share in the same unity and charity [n. 5].

Still another remarkable passage demonstrates a belief that a certain *de facto* unity has already occurred due to the common suffering encountered in the Second World War:

> Though a deadly and long war has pitilessly broken the bonds of brotherly union between nations, We have seen our children in Christ, in whatever part of the world they happened to be, with one heart and one affection lift up their souls to the common Father. . . . This is a testimony to the marvelous union existing among Christians [n. 6].

In 1949, the ecumenical monastic community of Taizé was founded by Brother Roger Schutz; it, too, continues its work, with a particular emphasis on a youth apostolate. Taizé is also well known for its beautiful chants, combining Latin (to foster unity even in language) and vernaculars.

Pius XII created the International Commission for Ecumenical Questions and appointed Msgr. Johannes Willebrands as its first chairman, which made 1952 a charter year for ecumenism. However much Pius XII did for unity by way of groundwork may never be known — although it was certainly done — but it all surfaced in 1960 when Pope John XXIII established the Secretariat for Christian Unity, by means of his decree *Superno Dei Nutu*. Whatever else had occurred in the Church's history, this showed the Catholic Church's commitment in a very concrete way to that dialogue that would bring about the unity so desired by Our Lord.

As the Catholic Church became convinced that ecumenical dialogue did not necessitate religious indifference, she threw her wholehearted support to the Christian-unity movement. With Catholic entrance as a serious participant and with the passage of time, Christians came together with increasing frequency and regularity — to meet, to pray, to study the Bible together — bringing us to the brink of Vatican II.

Vatican II

All of the events that were just rehearsed, however, were merely a foreshadowing of the events to follow as the great, decisive moment for ecumenism broke upon the world with the opening of the Second Vatican Council. For the first time since the Reformation, the Church did not feel threatened by secular culture or variant theological opinions but was open to them. Thus, it is obvious that the intense "dogmatization" of earlier councils gave the Church the security, identity, and self–awareness she needed to take the first steps toward unity — and this is significant. For all the criticism leveled at the Catholic Church for an alleged authoritarian absolutism, it must be remembered that the true initial movements toward unity have come from the See of Rome more than from any other communion.

Several documents of this Council were especially tailored to deal with matters related to ecumenism and interreligious affairs: *Unitatis Redintegratio* (Decree on Ecumenism) and *Nostra Aetate* (Declaration on the Relations of the Church to Non-Christian Religions), to be sure, but also *Ad Gentes Divinitus* (Decree on the Church's Missionary Activity) — all of which are treated in separate chapters in this volume. Critically important, too, was *Lumen Gentium* (Dogmatic Constitution on the Church), which provided the theological framework for these more "pastoral" documents.[37]

It is also interesting to note that in the documents of this Council there is an absence of the *anathemata* present in the documents of all other prior councils. Perhaps the dogmatic nature of Trent and Vatican I enabled Vatican II to develop a more "pastoral consciousness." Once again, however, we must underscore the need for dogma prior to pastoral theology: For theology without faith is meaningless, and faith without theology is blind.

Vatican II committed the Catholic Church to dialogue with all Christian communities, but the third chapter of *Unitatis Redintegratio* expresses the conviction that the greatest amount of ecumenical work (and success) can occur first with the Orthodox and Anglicans, and it is to these communions that we now turn our attention.

Dialogue With the Orthodox and Anglicans[38]

If Pope John XXIII is said to have set ecumenism in motion, Pope Paul VI kept ecumenism in this forward motion. His leadership with response to the Orthodox and Anglicans is especially noteworthy.

The year 1964 marked the historic meeting in Jerusalem between Pope Paul and Patriarch Athenagoras of Constantinople; the following year became famous in Catholic-Orthodox unity as the two men lifted the age-old mutual excommunications; in 1967 the two friends (and is this not a significant word to be able to use?) once again met and prayed together, this time in Constantinople. One observer rather perceptively read the "signs of the times" in noting that the "Decree on Ecumenism inaugurated a new phase in the history of Church movements for unity. Other initiatives of John XXIII and Paul VI have made it clear that this is no ephemeral change of climate but the entry into an authentically new era."[39] In this context, it is essential to recall how Pope John Paul II has, on numerous occasions, stressed the determination of the Catholic Church to stay the course.[40]

These personal encounters were by no means isolated events, as became evident from an ongoing series of such encounters. One thinks of the meeting on October 25, 1971, between Pope Paul and Mar Ignatius Jacob III, the Syrian-Orthodox Patriarch of Antioch, who remarked:

> Thank God those days of unhappy relations are now a thing of the past; and today there is real love and cooperation between our two Apostolic Sees, and Christian communions in general.

In the twentieth century there has never been a movement more fruitful than the ecumenical movement, and we
recognize with appreciation the constructive role Your Holiness' illustrious predecessor and your good self have played in
this field.[41]

That this is an "entry into an authentically new era" is evident in
the amount of progress that has been made through joint efforts of
the Catholic and Orthodox communions in permanent agencies.
The Ecumenical Patriarchate and the Catholic Church published a
folio in November 1970, in which all documents, letters, and speeches
affecting reciprocal relations were reprinted and submitted to the
Churches.

Relations with the Russian Orthodox advanced considerably
when Cardinal Willebrands was deputed to attend the funeral of
Patriarch Alexius as Pope Paul's personal representative. In December 1970, a discussion was held at Bari, Italy, in which Catholics and
Russian Orthodox considered "The Role of the Christian in the
Developing Society." The amazing degree of agreement in this crucial area was a source of great joy and hope for all participants.

After the historic visit of the Armenians' Supreme Catholicos,
Vasken I, to Pope Paul in May 1970, both Churches issued a declaration stressing the need for better communication and bearing more
fruitful witness to already existing bonds of unity.

The exchange of theological students between the Catholic West
and the Orthodox East has, as the Council foresaw, provided a mar-
velous source for dialogue and mutual friendship.[42]

A statement in a letter of Paul to Athenagoras contains two
striking phrases worthy of special consideration:

We reminded the faithful assembled in St. Peter's during
Unity Week that already *almost full communion* existed between
our Church and the venerated Orthodox Churches. Although
not yet perfect, this results from our *common participation in
the mystery of Christ and His Church* [emphasis added].[43]

Paul's obvious conviction in this regard is that we have almost arrived at complete unity, but important for our study is that it has come about from a "common participation in the mystery of . . . His Church." In other words, communion does exist, even if imperfect — the theological insight so carefully broached by Pope Pius XII in *Mystici Corporis* and then developed by the Fathers of Vatican II in *Lumen Gentium.* To commemorate the tenth anniversary of the lifting of the excommunications, Patriarch Dimitrios sent Metropolitan Meliton as his personal delegate to Pope Paul. In an astonishing act, Paul VI knelt down and kissed the feet of Meliton. Only the most astute historians caught the significance of it all: The Pope was symbolically attempting to reverse the situation after the Council of Florence when the Patriarch of Constantinople, Joseph II, was willing to return to Catholic unity but the Pope refused to dispense with the kissing of his foot then required by protocol.

Finally, Cardinal Willebrands seems to sum up Catholic-Orthodox relations very well in this passage:

> On the whole, therefore, one can see that our ecumenical activities in relation to the Oriental Churches differ quite extensively from occasion to occasion. At times we are concerned with festive and official visits, at others with private participations in important events in the life of the Church; sometimes the discussions revolve around topical questions and problems, at others they are designed to reflect about the official declarations of two Churches with a view to taking stock of the changes that have taken place in the relationships. . . . In all of this, however, we find a common denominator: the various steps and measures, of whatever kind they may be, grow directly out of the life of the Church; they are an expression of the growing communion among the Churches and are intended to serve the strengthening of this communion.[44]

Regrettably, much of the theological progress of the 1970s was undone at a practical level in the 1990s with the fall of communism and the subsequent conflicts between Eastern Catholic and Eastern Orthodox communities over ecclesiastical properties and the reemergence of the Eastern Catholic Churches after their forcible suppression under Stalin.

In regard to the Anglican Communion, the Permanent Anglican-Catholic International Commission was established, and its members worked with great diligence. A method of dialogue was outlined in a 1970 Vatican document, with the following suggestions given: exchange of ideas, comparison of ideas, research (e.g., What theological direction has been taken by the other Church since the break?), new insights or understandings, and work toward a constructive synthesis.[45] The greatest fruit of the commission's labors may have been the mutual publication of "position papers" of the two communions on the key areas of authority, ministry, and Eucharist.[46] Having had such great success in that first effort, the commission went on to approach the more tender and crucial topics of: the notion of sacrifice in the Anglican Eucharist, the Real Presence, and Eucharistic regulations.

Once more, however, much of the early progress was thwarted by other developments, especially the decision of the Anglican Communion to ordain women to the presbyterate and episcopate. Both Paul VI and John Paul II consistently warned the Anglican leadership that such moves would be detrimental to the dialogue and its goal of restoring full communion. Such counsel went unheeded.

In addition to these special opportunities for dialogue with Orthodoxy and Anglicanism, other theological conversations, both international and in the United States, have been most helpful to ecumenical understanding. Some of the American bilateral dialogues have had particularly positive results; one thinks of the following in this regard: Eastern Orthodox (begun in 1967), Coptic Orthodox (1973), Anglican Communion (1966), World Lutheran Federation (1967),[47] World Reformed Alliance (1970), World Methodist Council (1967), Disciples of Christ (1977), World Baptist Alliance (1984), Pentecostal groups (1971), and Evangelicals (1977).[48]

Conclusions

As early as 1962, Cardinal Giovanni Battista Montini (the future Pope Paul VI) with his usual prophetic foresight envisioned an entirely new age of unity emerging due to the Council:

> If the Council does not succeed in celebrating the return of the separated brethren, it will at least succeed in opening the doors of the family home to them, in smoothing the way, in sending out its warm appeal for their reintegration into the one truly apostolic Catholic Church. Ecumenism will become an integral part of the Church's *desires* and *prayers* and *structure*. This will be a great thing for the world's peace and for establishing the spiritual foundation without which union between nations becomes so difficult and precarious [emphasis added].[49]

At the very beginning of his pontificate, Blessed Pope John pleaded, "Let us look at each other without mistrust, meet each other without fear, talk to each other without surrendering principle."[50] Among the virtues of ecumenism, we may cite the following: "Faith and confidence, perseverance, hope and patience are essential parts of this work. In this connection, moreover, the word 'patience' does not stand for a merely passive expectancy; it stands for a truly Christian virtue that never gives up, that never tires, because it is founded on faith and confidence and draws its security from these."[51]

All of the above statements indicate how we should approach unity. A large problem that cannot be adequately treated here but must nevertheless be at least mentioned is *"communicate in sacris"* (that is, intercommunion.) The Catholic Church (like the Orthodox Churches) has reacted negatively to this prospect, on the grounds that the Eucharist is the highest symbol of unity; thus, where true unity does not exist, celebrating a common Eucharist becomes a counter-sign and may actually be seen as ecumenically counterproductive since, in a very direct sense, it places the cart before the horse.

Sloppy or sentimental ecumenism is not good ecumenism. One need only reflect on the fact that so many non-Catholic Christian communities that entered into agreements of eucharistic sharing decades ago (on the presumption and in the hope that such intercommunion would facilitate organic unity) are no closer to genuine reunion than when they started and, in many cases, are even farther apart, objectively speaking. Sensing the pain of disunity can be a most salutary goad to invest one's time and talents in the quest for the unity to which the Holy Spirit calls us. The Methodist scholar Thomas C. Oden, in reflecting on his participation in Pope John Paul II's Mass in the papal chapel, offers these insightful and faith-filled words:

> I was pretty sure I would be the only non-Roman Catholic at the pope's private mass. And I was. I did not receive Communion. So I now ponder the Supper I missed. I did indeed miss it, not by design or intent but because I respect the Roman Catholic canon law tradition. I would gladly have received it. Honestly, my soul thirsted for it, but I bypassed receiving the body and blood of Christ from the pope's own hands. Why? Because I am not a baptized Roman Catholic. Even though I am baptized in the one, holy, catholic, apostolic church, there is doubt on the part of some of the oneness and catholicity of my baptism. I consoled myself with the thought that I am far more catholic than some of my protestantizing, hypermodern, experimentalist Roman Catholic theological colleagues. No, I have not been through Roman Catholic catechetics, though I think I could pass an examination on the subject. I was not duly prepared according to canon law to come forward, though I would have been inwardly ready to come. I did not have the proper wedding garment for this celebration. Yet, no one there turned me away except myself.[52]

Christian unity is not a luxury for the Church; it is a necessity, willed by Christ, and the Catholic Church sees herself as especially responsible for leading the way in this matter in her role as the "church which presides over all the others in charity."[53] Echoing these sentiments, Pope John Paul II spoke thus to the cardinals of the Roman Curia on June 28, 1985 (commemorating the twentieth anniversary of the final session of Vatican II):

> This movement comes from the Holy Spirit, and I feel deeply responsible to Him. I humbly ask for His light and His strength so as better to serve this holy cause of unity. I ask you to implore this grace with me, to implore it for me. I would repeat that it is with an irrevocable decision of the Catholic Church that it became involved in the ecumenical movement and that she wishes to contribute to it in every way she can. As Bishop of Rome, I consider it one of my pastoral priorities.

CHAPTER THREE

Unitatis Redintegratio
(Decree on Ecumenism)

"THE RESTORATION OF UNITY among all Christians is one of the principal concerns of the Second Vatican Council" (n. 1), begins the Decree on Ecumenism (*Unitatis Redintegratio*), approved by the bishops on November 21, 1964.

The Council Fathers open their reflections in an orderly and positive manner, with Christian unity presented as the goal, grounded in the unity of the Blessed Trinity, "the highest exemplar and source of this mystery" (n. 2) and rooted in the Lord's High Priestly Prayer for His Church on the night before He died, "that they may all be one" (Jn 17:21).

Acknowledging today's lack of Christian unity, the bishops declare that "such division openly contradicts the will of Christ" (n. 1), scandalizes the world, and harms the cause of the Gospel. They base this assertion on St. John's reason for the priority of unity: "that they may all be one . . . so that the world may believe that thou hast sent me" (Jn 17:21).

According to John, the advancement of the Gospel is inhibited by the fragmented witness of a divided Church. The bishops conclude, therefore, that divine inspiration undergirds the ecumenical movement, which they define as efforts toward unity on the part of those who invoke the Triune God and confess Jesus as Lord and Savior.

Thus, technically speaking, ecumenism involves *only Christians* engaged in building religious unity. In common parlance, of course, ecumenism has come to mean an attitude of openness toward all faiths (Christian or not) — but that kind of activity was the topic of a completely separate conciliar document, for both practical and theological reasons.

Before embarking on a study of disunion and its healing, the decree notes that the Council "has already declared its teaching on the Church" (n. 1) in *Lumen Gentium* and "now . . . wishes to set before all Catholics guidelines, helps and methods" for such ecumenical activity. It is important to notice the wording of this statement and especially the order of the phrasing. The bishops say that, having explained Catholic ecclesiology, they are now in a position to provide suggestions for Catholic participation in the ecumenical movement. In other words, the Decree on Ecumenism is entirely dependent on the Dogmatic Constitution on the Church.

This is crucial because so much confusion has resulted from a failure to appreciate the dependency of Catholic ecumenism on a thoroughly Catholic ecclesiology. Doctrines of apostolic succession and papal primacy, for example, are not "up for grabs" in ecumenical conversations because *Lumen Gentium* has unambiguously held them to be at the very heart of our ecclesial life. Further on in the decree, the bishops do say, however, that Catholics must make such doctrines intelligible to other Christians.

The decree next takes a historical approach, noting that division is not, unfortunately, a new phenomenon among Christians. In fact, disunity is found right in the New Testament, where we read of St. Paul's condemnations of that contentiousness that breaks the bond of unity in Christ. With the passage of time, more serious rifts in the Christian community developed, "for which often enough, men of both sides were to blame" (n. 3).

This striking admission that the Council Fathers accept some responsibility for Christian disunity was a point returned to by Pope John Paul II in his homily at the Lutheran church in Rome on the occasion commemorating the five-hundredth anniversary of the birth of Martin Luther.

While disunity is a sign of sin among members of the sinless Body of Christ, "one cannot charge with the sin of separation those who at present are born into these communities and in them are brought up in the faith of Christ." On the contrary, assert the bishops, "the Catholic Church accepts them with respect and affection as brothers" (n. 3). The reason for this acceptance lies in our awareness that through Baptism, all Christians are put in some, though imperfect, communion with the Catholic Church (cf. n. 3).

This "imperfect communion" results from the theological conviction that "some, even very many, of the most significant elements and endowments which together go to build up and give life to the Church itself, can exist outside the visible boundaries of the Catholic Church" (n. 3). These elements include: the Word of God, the life of grace, and certain visible structures. This is a very balanced presentation of Catholic teaching on non-Catholic Christians. Such believers have a genuine relationship with Jesus Christ, so that what unites us can become foundational for healing what divides us. At the same time, they do not enjoy the fullness of truth found "through Christ's Catholic Church alone" (n. 3).

In keeping with this line of thought, the decree teaches that these separated Churches and ecclesial communities, although defective, "have been by no means deprived of significance and importance in the mystery of salvation," but that they "derive their efficacy" from the Catholic Church (n. 3). Theological accuracy, and not mere verbiage, causes the Council Fathers repeatedly to refer to "Churches *and communities*" because these are two different realities. "Churches" are those bodies that have retained apostolic succession and, therefore, Holy Orders and a valid Eucharist. The decree grants a quasi-churchly status to other Christian groups ("communities") that lack those dimensions.

Some may take offense at the conciliar declaration that these other Christian bodies "derive their efficacy" from the Catholic Church; however, this is but one more example of how *Lumen Gentium* undergirds *Unitatis Redintegratio*.

After years of what can only be called "foot-dragging," the Church comes out in this decree in full support of the ecumenical movement, urging Catholics "to recognize the signs of the times and to take an active and intelligent part in the work of ecumenism" (n. 4). The bishops outline the agenda for such a program: the "effort to avoid expressions, judgments and actions which do not represent the condition of our separated brethren with truth and fairness," thus keeping away from those things that make relations more difficult; " 'dialogue' between competent experts"; "intensive cooperation . . . for the common good of humanity"; "common prayer"; and the communal and personal task of "renewal and reform." All of this is to be "carried out by the Catholic faithful with prudent patience and under the attentive guidance of their bishops" (n. 4).

Furthermore, Catholics must be concerned for their "separated brethren," pray for them, and keep them informed about the Church and also must "make a careful and honest appraisal of whatever needs to be renewed and done in the Catholic household itself" to enhance its life and witness (no. 4).

This final item for the Catholic agenda holds true because "Christ summons the Church . . . to that continual reformation of which she always has need" (n. 5). This reformation of the body, however, can occur only insofar as it takes place in the members who "try to live holier lives," for there can be "no ecumenism worthy of the name without interior conversion" (n. 7).

The Council Fathers speak of this aspect of ecumenical activity as "spiritual ecumenism," which consists in a "change of heart," "holiness of life," and "public and private prayer for the unity of Christians" (n. 8). Excluded from such public prayer, however, is "*communicatio in sacris*," or forms of official, liturgical prayer that might give the impression that full unity already exists. This means that "intercommunion" is usually prohibited, although it *is* possible to some limited degree with the separated Churches of the East (cf. n. 15).

The decree calls for dialogue by which we "become familiar with the outlook of our separated brethren . . . [through] meetings of the two sides" (n. 9), bringing about clarification for both. Theology should be taught "with due regard for the ecumenical point of view" (n. 10), which is to say that history should be taken seriously and presented honestly.

At the same time, the bishops denounce every form of "false irenicism," which would attempt to show unity where it does not truly exist or to gloss over important differences in such a way as to suggest that they are unimportant. A properly open attitude will, however, keep in mind that Catholic doctrine admits of a " 'hierarchy of truths" (n. 11), in which some teachings lie closer to the heart of the matter than others.

Thus, in conversations with our separated brothers and sisters, it is necessary to bear in mind that the Real Presence of Christ in the Eucharist and devotion to Our Lady of Fátima are not held or taught with equal intensity. The Council Fathers advocate "cooperation in social matters" among all Christians (n. 12) as a means of serving humanity by a united witness and as a way of getting to know one another in activities not designed to highlight conflict, thus paving the way for more serious theological discussions.

In a brief survey of the chief divisions in the Christian family, the bishops pay particular attention to the Churches of the East and the communities separated from Rome at the time of the Protestant Reformation. Much time is spent discussing the Eastern Churches, affirming their full ecclesial status in the eyes of the Catholic Church and assuring them that, should they accept the invitation to reunion with the See of Rome, they will "have the power to govern themselves according to their own disciplines" (n. 16), even if this has not always been so in the past.

In considering the Reformation communities, the "Anglican Communion" is singled out for special notice. While giving due attention to the bonds of unity between Catholics and Christians of the Reformation, the Council Fathers do not shy away from stating that "very weighty differences" (n. 19) exist between Catholics and Protestants and, furthermore, among the various Protestant communities themselves (a point we often forget). The bishops encourage theological dialogues with these groups and suggest that such dialogues "could start with the moral application of the Gospel" (n. 23).

It is interesting that bilateral discussions with the Orthodox, Anglicans, and Lutherans have been particularly fruitful, while social cooperation on matters of public policy has sometimes been more worthwhile between Catholics and Fundamentalists, especially in the

United States. Nevertheless, it is also sadly necessary to note that since the promulgation of the decree, a loss of consensus on various moral issues (like abortion) between Catholics and mainline Protestants now militates against the goal expressed in the document.

Although firm in the desire for full unity among Christians, the decree "urges the faithful to abstain from any frivolous or imprudent zeal" because every ecumenical activity must be "loyal to the truth" (n. 24).

The bishops end on a hopeful note in their appraisal of where the ecumenical movement will lead, because they view Christian unity as the will of Christ and the work of the Holy Spirit. Repeatedly throughout his pontificate, John Paul II has used an interesting phrase to describe the Catholic position on ecumenism; he speaks of the Church at Vatican II as having made an "irrevocable commitment." This is strong language, requiring equally strong action on the part of every Catholic.

A clear course was set by the Council, consisting of a two-part program: (1) work, study, and action, as if to suggest that everything depended on us, and (2) prayer, as if to suggest that everything depended on God. That combination is unbeatable, for it is the very one God has always used to work His greatest miracles. Somewhat presciently, Father Thomas Stransky saw the direction that *Unitatis Redintegratio* would demand when he wrote nearly forty years ago that "the decree is a charter for a movement, not an absolute crystallization of a static position."[54]

CHAPTER FOUR

~~

Nostra Aetate
(Declaration on the Relations of the Church to Non-Christian Religions)

PROCLAIMING THE BASIC UNITY of the human family and the belief that religion should always strengthen that natural unity, the Fathers of the Second Vatican Council issued *Nostra Aetate*, the Declaration on the Relations of the Church to Non-Christian Religions (promulgated on October 28, 1965), which reflects "on what men have in common and what tends to promote fellowship among them" (n. 1).

With the conviction that all religions should help answer the fundamental questions of life, the declaration asserts that "the Catholic Church rejects nothing of what is true and holy in these religions" (n. 2). And this statement is the basis for Pope Paul VI's subsequent discussion, in his apostolic exhortation *Evangelii Nuntiandi*, of how even primitive religions can serve as a "preparation for the Gospel" by readying people's hearts for the fullness of salvation that comes through Jesus Christ.

Nostra Aetate surveys the various approaches to God found in the religions of the world, with special notice given to Hinduism and Buddhism because of their antiquity, their elevated spiritual values, and the vast number of adherents they claim. The Council Fathers also speak approvingly of all religions that, by creed, code, and cult, strive to lead human beings to respond to the promptings of the natural law and the innate desire for union with the Supreme Being.

Also singled out for consideration are the Muslims, who, as a "People of the Book" along with Jews and Christians, adore the one true God, acknowledge Jesus as a prophet, venerate His holy mother, await the final judgment, and look for the resurrection of the dead. Acknowledging a history of tension between Muslims and Christians, the declaration issues a plea to forget past injuries and to make a commitment for mutual understanding in the future — points reprised by Pope John Paul II in his historic visits to Morocco in 1985 and to Syria in 2001.

It needs to be noted, however, that in spite of expressing great esteem for the various religions of the world, nowhere does *Nostra Aetate* endorse a kind of religious indifferentism or false irenicism, which would view all religions as equal. The declaration, in fact, states quite clearly that the Church "is in duty bound to proclaim without fail, Christ who is the way, the truth and the life (Jn 1:6). In him, in whom God reconciled all things to himself (2 Cor 5:18-19), men find the fullness of their religious life" (n. 2). This teaching must be understood as a foundation stone in any interfaith dialogue and most especially by those engaged in missionary work, whose ultimate goal must always be to bring people to "find the fullness of their religious life," a fullness found only in Jesus Christ.

The rest of the document is devoted to the Jews. It is not an accident that the man regarded as the principal architect of this section was an Austrian-born Jewish convert, Msgr. John Oesterreicher, founder of the internationally respected Institute of Judeo-Christian Studies at Seton Hall University. Msgr. Oesterreicher tried to offer his life and witness as a bridge between the Jewish and Christian communities, reminding both of their "common spiritual heritage" and encouraging them toward "further mutual understanding and appreciation" (n. 4).

In quick succession, the Council Fathers tackle some of the more thorny problems of Jewish-Christian relations, as well as popular misunderstandings of Catholic belief. In spite of the fact that Marcion was declared a heretic for his negative assessment of the Old Testament and its heritage, some Jews and some Christians throughout the centuries since have assumed that Marcion's error somehow has validity in the Catholic community. *Nostra Aetate* rejects any such view. Regarding the charge of "deicide" by the complicity of some Jews in the death of Jesus, the declaration reminds all that Jesus went to His death freely and in love; that some Jews did indeed reject Jesus and called for His death, while others became His loyal followers; that no collective responsibility can be ascribed to the Jewish people and surely no eternal curse, for "the Jews remain very dear to God" (n. 4). Finally, the bishops proclaim that "the Church reproves every form of persecution against whomsoever it may be directed," including "displays of anti-Semitism leveled at any time or from any source against the Jews" (n. 4).

As far back as 1959, the Jewish scholar Jules Isaac in *Jesus and Israel* made a plea for Christians to come to a deeper appreciation of the Jewish roots of their faith. In many ways, *Nostra Aetate* is an endorsement of Isaac's insights. John Paul II, in a meeting with leaders of the Jewish community in France, identified Isaac as a "pioneer" in "the movement that has led us to the present dialogue and collaboration," due to his "courage and decision." The Pope went on to note the depth of the relationship between Judaism and the Church as one "at the very level of their respective religious identities." Of course, in many ways this observation was merely a paraphrase of Pope Pius XI's axiom that all Christians are and need to be "religious Semites."

What is the unfinished agenda for Jewish-Catholic relations nearly forty years after this declaration? We should begin by noting how well our preachers and catechists have implemented the desires of the Council Fathers by eliminating false images of Jews or Judaism. Catholics still need to be reminded from time to time of their Jewish religious heritage and most especially that Judaism is not a bankrupt or forsaken religion — as St. Paul takes great pains to observe. Ways also need to be found to promote in an organized and ongoing manner the "mutual understanding" called for by the Council.

That said, Catholics have a right to expect similar responses from the Jewish community. But this has sometimes been lacking, creating the impression of a one-way dialogue. Our encounter with Judaism, moreover, is complicated by the existence of very diverse schools of Jewish thought and no one authoritative voice to engage in the dialogue. Thus, when Catholics seek Jewish support for anti-abortion legislation or governmental programs to aid parochial school children, their overtures are usually rebuffed by secularized Jews and the more "liberal" segments of religious Jewry; only Orthodox Jews seem to share our social vision and goals. At the same time, many Jews cannot comprehend why Catholics insist on a vindication of the rights of the Palestinians. Catholics are similarly offended when some Jews speak of "twenty centuries of Christian anti-Semitism," as though such prejudice were officially endorsed and encouraged by the Church. Even more difficult to understand is the tendency of some Jews to blame the Nazi Holocaust on the Church — and most particularly on Pope Pius XII, suggesting a kind of "Jewish anti-Catholicism."

These negative elements, of course, should never be allowed to dampen the spirit of goodwill engendered by *Nostra Aetate*. Rather, they are part of the road yet to be walked by two communities that look for the day of the Messiah's coming in glory — on a day we will greet each other as brothers and sisters because of the common Father we worship.

CHAPTER FIVE

～

Ad Gentes Divinitus
(Decree on the Church's Missionary Activity)

POPE JOHN'S COUNCIL WAS UNIQUE for its openness to the world, and this was especially highlighted in its Decree on the Church's Missionary Activity, promulgated on December 7, 1965.

Even the document's Latin title (*Ad Gentes* — "to the nations" — *Divinitus*) stresses this outward thrust, which then carries forward in statements like "The Church on earth is by its very nature missionary" (n. 2). The Church is "divinely sent" to engage in missionary activity, and this work is "demanded by her own essential universality," for the "kingdom of God [must be] proclaimed and renewed throughout the whole world" (n. 1).

Catholic missionary work is rooted in a twofold love of God and neighbor. How so? "Missionary activity is nothing else, and nothing less, than the manifestation of God's plan, its epiphany and realization in the world and in history" (n. 9). Similarly, "in manifesting Christ, the Church reveals to men their true situation and calling" (n. 8), "so that what was accomplished for the salvation of all men may, in the course of time, achieve its universal effect" (n. 3). Looking at the billions of human souls in the world and realizing how so many have never even heard the name of Jesus Christ, the bishops declare that "tremendous missionary work still remains to be done" (n. 10).

In recent years, some confusion has occurred over what constitutes "authentic" missionary activity. No such ambiguity, however, exists in this document. "Its aim is to open up for all men a free and sure path to full participation in the mystery of Christ" (n. 5), for there is no " 'salvation in any other' (Acts 4:12)" (n. 7). So much for those who claim that Vatican II downplayed the need for conversion!

On the contrary, we find an explicit statement that "the special end of this missionary activity is the evangelization and the implanting of the Church among peoples or groups in which it has not yet taken root" (n. 6). Of course, missionaries must respect local customs, culture, and traditions — but they must likewise endeavor to "[raise] them to a catholic perfection" (n. 6), which is to say that every culture — no matter how sophisticated — is in need of evangelization. Concerning the unevangelized, the Council offers this reflection:

> So, although in ways known to himself God can lead those who, through no fault of their own, are ignorant of the Gospel to that faith without which it is impossible to please him (Heb. 11:6), the Church, nevertheless, still has the obligation and also the sacred right to evangelize. And so, today as always, missionary activity retains its full force and necessity [n. 7].

When the Gospel cannot be preached directly, "missionaries, patiently, prudently, and with great faith, can and ought at least bear witness to the love and kindness of Christ and thus prepare a way for the Lord, and in some way make him present" (n. 6). This is done through the Church's works of charity, which are "extended to all without distinction of race, social condition, or religion, and seek neither gain nor gratitude." Schools are singled out for particular praise, but the bishops also note that Christian charity may never have for its goal a "merely material progress." As regards political activity, the Council Fathers bluntly assert that "the Church . . . has no desire to become involved in the government of the temporal order" (n. 12).

"Since the whole Church is missionary," every Catholic has a role to play in evangelization: bishops, clergy, Religious, and laity. Common to all believers is the need to "foster . . . a truly Catholic spirit," to "lead a profound Christian life," to pray and do penance for the success of mission efforts, and to support the use of modern means of communication for the spread of the Gospel (n. 35). Bishops, in particular, are reminded of the necessity of being mission-minded: "The grace of renewal cannot grow in communities unless each of them expands the range of its charity to the ends of the earth, and has the same concern for those who are far away as it has for its own members" (n. 37). This principle is based on yet another fact: "Both Christ and the Church which bears witness to him transcend the distinctions of race and nationality, and so cannot be considered as strangers to anyone or in any place" (n. 8).

Chapter V is devoted to the kind of planning essential for fruitful missionary endeavors, which must always move forward under the direction of the local bishop "as the head . . . and center of unity" in a diocese (n. 30). The training of seminarians (n. 16) and catechists (n. 17) receives careful attention. The Council Fathers refuse to back away from their view that *all* believers must be involved in missionary work, even when discussing missionary orders, "who take on the duty of evangelization, which pertains to the whole Church" (n. 23); in other words, these members of the Church fulfill a kind of surrogate role, which can never be completely handed over to them in such a manner as to absolve the rest of the Church from its responsibility in this sphere.

A full-time "professional" missionary, however, does have a special vocation as Christ's "legate," who must never be "ashamed of the scandal of the Cross" and who must be willing to witness, "if necessary to the shedding of his blood" (n. 24). Thus, the missionary requires "special spiritual and moral formation" (n. 25), which should be completed in the lands to which he or she will be sent. That training should seek to provide the ability to "understand both the universality of the Church and the diversity of peoples" (n. 26).

The great esteem in which the Church holds religious life shines through when we read that "right from the planting of the Church the religious life should be carefully fostered," not only because of the assistance Religious provide for mission work but most especially because religious life shows forth the Church in a unique way (n. 18). *Ad Gentes Divinitus* builds on *Lumen Gentium*'s recognition of the importance of the laity by noting that "the Church is not truly established and does not fully live, nor is it a perfect sign of Christ unless there is a genuine laity existing and working alongside the hierarchy." In addition to the vital work of catechesis, lay people are urged to make use of their "social and professional ties" for the good of the Church. Thus, clergy and laity together will "bear a simple, living, strong witness" (n. 21).

Much is said about a vibrant catechumenate, which exists not only to provide detailed information about the Christian Faith, but also to purify motives for conversion, and never to force or pressure people into the Church (cf. n. 13). The bishops observe that Lent and Easter should be celebrated in such a way that their ancient character of preparation for reception into the Church can be reemphasized by "successive sacred rites" (n. 14). This has subsequently been accomplished in the establishment of the Rite of Christian Initiation of Adults (RCIA). The document also urges that a clear definition of a catechumen be provided for in the revision of the Church's law, which has likewise been accomplished.

In considering those places where the seed of the Gospel is newly sown, *Ad Gentes Divinitus* makes a number of important observations. First, these "young churches" will need continued missionary assistance, both in clergy and in finances. Second, it should be a goal to bring them to provide for themselves as quickly as possible and even to send out missionaries of their own, which is now happening as numerous "first world" dioceses are receiving and even becoming dependent on large numbers of clergy and Religious from newly evangelized countries; this phenomenon Pope John Paul II has often referred to as "an exchange of gifts," inasmuch as the developed Western nations often brought the Faith to these peoples who are now living it so intently as to be able to assist us who have apparently lost our moorings. Third, these mission territories should have their own "hierarchy" (cf. n. 6), a development which has occurred with amazing speed and with generally very positive results in terms of quality. Finally, "the communion of the young churches with the whole Church must remain intimate," with healthy interaction and for mutual enrichment (n. 19).

An ecumenical note is interjected as the bishops remind all that "the division of Christians is injurious to the holy work of preaching the Gospel to every creature" (n. 6). The hope, then, is that the future task of evangelization will be made more effective by the witness of a united Church.

While the Council Fathers salute "all preachers of the Gospel," they make special mention of those "who suffer persecution for the name of Christ" (n. 42). In this way, they recall the close connection between Christian witness and persecution, both of which translate from the Greek word *martyros* — a sober thought for so many of us who have grown comfortable in our Christianity.

As children in grammar school, we learned of the universality of the Church and the need for positive action to see that the Gospel would indeed be preached to the very ends of the earth. Daily prayer for the missions and "adopting pagan babies" formed the core of our work. In our contemporary smugness, we may smile at "mite boxes" and christening pagan babies, but the closing point of *Ad Gentes Divinitus* was made — very strongly — long before the closing prayer of the decree was written: "That the glory of God, which shines in the face of Jesus Christ, might shed its light on all men through the Holy Spirit" (n. 42).

"Keeping the Faith" is not enough; *spreading* it is required. In fact, those who do not spread the Faith are in danger of losing it. Simply put, that is the message of *Ad Gentes Divinitus* — and of the whole Second Vatican Council.

CHAPTER SIX

Dignitatis Humanae
(Declaration on Religious Liberty)

WHEN THE DECLARATION ON RELIGIOUS LIBERTY (promulgated on December 7, 1965) is discussed, commentators usually note that among the most influential figures in its drafting were an American priest and a Polish bishop — one from the freest land in the world and the other from behind the Iron Curtain.

The American had lived under a cloud for many years because of his notions of religion in a free culture, ideas that sounded alien to European Catholic ears used to civil societies intertwined with religion. Cardinal Francis Spellman of New York nonetheless brought Jesuit Father John Courtney Murray to Rome for the Council, to share with the Church his reconciliation of democracy, religious liberty, and Catholic truth.

His Polish counterpart was a philosophy professor and a recently consecrated bishop, Karol Wojtyla of Kraków — now Pope John Paul II — who sought to express in clear terms the necessity of religious freedom and the philosophical rationale behind it.

"Contemporary man is becoming increasingly conscious of the dignity of the human person," begins the declaration (n. 1), which appropriately takes for its official title the document's first two words in Latin: *Dignitatis Humanae*. Religious liberty is thus firmly grounded in "the dignity of the human person."

This approach bears the distinctive imprint of the young Wojtyla, whose philosophy of personalism is only now becoming better known. This school of philosophy sees rights and obligations flowing not from norms external to man but as a response to the great dignity of human nature. For this reason, the Council Fathers declare that religious freedom is a fundamental "civil right" (n. 2), a teaching which they locate in Divine Revelation and human reason.

The declaration first speaks of religious liberty in negative terms by indicating what would constitute violations of this right: The human person "must not be forced to act contrary to his conscience. Nor must he be prevented from acting according to his conscience, especially in religious matters . . . because the practice of religion of its very nature consists primarily of those voluntary and free internal acts by which a man directs himself to God. Acts of this kind cannot be commanded or forbidden by any merely human authority" (n. 3).

On the positive side, the bishops outline the several rights of religious individuals and communities: the right of belief and practice; the right not to be hindered in the selection and appointment of individuals to fill ministerial roles; the right to communicate with co-religionists in other lands; the right to purchase property and build edifices for religious purposes; the right to be free to engage in public teaching and in demonstrating the value of religion to society-at-large (cf. n. 4). The Council Fathers also stress the need for religious individuals to form associations and communities.

Dignitatis Humanae argues that "the protection and promotion of the inviolable rights of man is an essential duty of every civil authority." Conversely, the repression of religion is a "transgression of God's will and of the sacred rights of the individual person and the family of nations" (n. 6). Logically, then, the bishops conclude that "the freedom of the Church is the fundamental principle governing relations between the Church and public authorities and the whole civil order" (n. 13).

According to the Council, is it possible for religious liberty to prosper in an environment other than the American? Yes, even in nations that have an established, or state, religion, provided that "the right of all citizens and religious communities . . . [is] recognized and respected as well" (n. 6). Examples would be England (where the Church of England is the state religion) or Italy (which has, in the past, accorded a special status to Catholicism, without establishment). In both instances, however, complete freedom of religion exists for all, believers or not.

The Council Fathers also turn their attention to more subtle forms of religious discrimination as they arise in the education context:

> The civil authority must therefore recognize the right of parents to choose with genuine freedom schools or other means of education. Parents should not be subjected directly or indirectly to unjust burdens because of this freedom of choice. Furthermore, the rights of parents are violated if their children are compelled to attend classes which are not in agreement with the religious beliefs of the parents or if there is but a single compulsory system of education from which all religious instruction is excluded [n. 5].

Father Murray had argued this point eloquently five years earlier in his classic on religious freedom, *We Hold These Truths*. But decades after Vatican II, few U.S. Catholics yet perceive the injustice inflicted by the American system of education and educational funding; even fewer have attempted to do something politically to remedy the injustice.

Always realistic, the declaration also notes that "civil society has the right to protect itself against possible abuses committed in the name of religious freedom" (n. 7). Sects that promote anarchy or immorality under the guise of religion come to mind immediately, as well as groups that prey on the young or impressionable to achieve their ends.

One of dissident Archbishop Marcel Lefebvre's principal objections to *Dignitatis Humanae* was that the document grants rights to those in error. The Council deals with this issue in a very nuanced manner. Thus, we read that "all men are bound to seek the truth, especially in what concerns God and His Church, and to embrace it and hold on to it as they come to know it" (n. 1). But how does this happen? "Truth can impose itself on the mind of man only in virtue of its own truth, which wins over the mind with both gentleness and power" (n. 1). Thus, it is necessary "to treat with love, prudence and patience those who are in error or ignorance with regard to the faith" (n. 14).

The declaration clearly teaches that objective truth does exist and can be known, but that the truth cannot be imparted through force or fear. Hence, the bishops declare that "religious freedom in society is in complete harmony with the act of Christian faith . . . [which holds] that man's response to God by faith ought to be free" (nn. 9-10). It is this very point that Lefebvre found most offensive, operating under the ancient dictum that "error has no rights" and pointing to past Church actions and attitudes on this issue. The bishops face the objection squarely, and the historical record as well, admitting that "although . . . there has at times appeared a form of behavior which was hardly in keeping with the spirit of the Gospel and was even opposed to it, it has always remained the teaching of the Church that no one is to be coerced into believing" (n. 12). In this statement, we find a striking example of honesty coupled with a strong doctrinal commitment to religious liberty.

What is the appropriate American response to *Dignitatis Humanae*, nearly forty years later? First of all, we should thank Almighty God for the freedom that is our heritage. Second, we must exercise our religious rights to the full and press for those rights not yet possessed. Third, we should remember that millions of our brothers and sisters throughout the world still do not enjoy religious liberty. Therefore, we must help those who cannot help themselves by using all means of politics and diplomacy, that these too may serve God fully and openly.

Finally, and most importantly, we should unite ourselves with them in prayer to the Father of all, Who endows His children with the desire to worship Him — a desire that corresponds to, and reveals, both their human dignity and their divine calling.

CHAPTER SEVEN

Orientalium Ecclesiarum
(Decree on the Catholic Eastern Churches)

"Variety is the spice of life," sums up the theme of *Orientalium Ecclesiarum*, Vatican II's Decree on the Catholic Eastern Churches (promulgated on November 21, 1964). The document is directed to a variety of audiences: the Universal Church, the Eastern Churches, and the Latin (or Roman) rite.

Most Catholics who have grown up in the United States do not have the vaguest idea of what Eastern-rite Catholics are — or that they even exist. This is unfortunate, because it suggests that most of us operate from a very poor and narrow ecclesiology.

The Dogmatic Constitution on the Church stresses that the Universal Church is a communion of local churches. Within the bounds imposed by the unity of faith, the Church has traditionally encouraged the expression of that faith in ways best suited to local culture, especially in liturgy and discipline. As history was played out, these "local expressions" clustered around certain large ecclesiastical centers, eventually designated as patriarchates. The way the liturgy was celebrated in such a center came to be known as a *rite*.

In the East, vernacular languages were regularly used for the liturgy, or at least sacred languages that were close enough to the vernacular that they were generally comprehensible to the worshiping community. In the West, liturgical variations were subsumed into the Roman rite very early on, with some important exceptions (e.g., the Dominican, Mozarabic, and Ambrosian rites). As a result, Latin and the rubrics of Rome were used for the whole Western Church.

In addition to language, certain disciplinary differences existed between East and West as well. The most notable was the observance of celibacy. In both East and West, celibacy was always highly esteemed, but the West took the scriptural ideal of celibacy and made it normative. The East, on the other hand, indicated its preference for celibacy by requiring men opting for marriage to do so *before* ordination, with the clear understanding that they could not remarry should they be widowed. Further, only celibate clergy (or monks) would be considered for the episcopacy.[55]

This brief historical overview may help us better appreciate the conciliar decree. Sometimes Latin-rite Catholics wonder why a Church that values unity so highly would permit such diversity. The point to remember, however, is that the differences among the rites in no way relate to matters of faith and morals. Therefore, the Church lives by this ancient principle: "In necessary things, unity; in doubtful things, liberty; in all things, charity."

Thus, we read that "between those churches [or rites] there is such a wonderful communion that this variety, so far from diminishing the Church's unity, rather serves to emphasize it" (n. 2). Unity can obviously be maintained without uniformity.

Because the Latin rite is the largest, and because the Bishop of Rome guides the entire Church, the impression can occur that the Roman rite is superior to all others. But the Council Fathers reject any such view by declaring that all rites are "of equal rank" (n. 3). They also stress that in all matters not directly touching on the unity of the Faith, the various rites have "the right and duty to govern themselves" (n. 5). It should be noted that the Pope as "universal pastor" is "omni-ritual" (i.e., able to celebrate the liturgy in every rite), and that the Eastern Churches live under their own separate Code of Canon Law.

Because of Roman influence (at times, not well or charitably used), some Eastern Churches experienced strong tendencies to "Latinize" their liturgical life. Distinct features of Eastern liturgy were unfortunately discarded and replaced with Western forms or nothing at all — altar rails (instead of icon screens) and statues (instead of icons) are the obvious examples. To stem this tide, the Council Fathers urged the Eastern Churches "to strive to return to their ancestral traditions" (n. 6). Sometimes Latin-rite Catholics express pleasure that the local Eastern-rite parish is getting "just like us." But this is not a cause for rejoicing, because the beauty of the Church shines forth best when legitimate diversity is fostered, reflecting the many peoples and cultures that share the Faith. As a result of the decree, many Eastern-rite bishops have led their people to a renewed appreciation of their own unique tradition and with strong encouragement from Rome in the post-conciliar era.

The Council Fathers next consider the schism between East and West, which was finalized in 1054 when the patriarchs of the East (Constantinople) and West (Rome) mutually excommunicated each other. As a result, Orthodox Christians do not acknowledge the authority of the Pope and thus for more than nine centuries have not partaken in Catholic unity.

The bishops call on Eastern Catholics to make themselves a bridge between Catholics and Orthodox since they (as Catholics) accept the Bishop of Rome yet simultaneously share the same liturgical and disciplinary traditions as the Orthodox, not to mention the same spirituality and culture: "The Eastern Churches in communion with the Apostolic See of Rome have the special duty of fostering the unity of all Christians, in particular of Eastern Christians" (n. 24).

The bishops also indicate that when "access to a Catholic priest is physically or morally impossible," Catholics may validly and licitly receive the Sacraments of Penance, Holy Eucharist, and Anointing of the Sick from an Orthodox priest, since Orthodox Orders are valid (n. 27). Further, Orthodox in similar situations may seek the same sacraments from a Catholic priest (cf. n. 28). In this instance, ironically, Roman law is more "liberal" than Orthodox law, which frowns on such practices because the Orthodox consider Catholics to be lacking the true Faith, and hence not in communion with them.

The Council Fathers put forth their ecumenical guidelines "in view of present conditions, until such time as the Catholic Church and the separated Eastern Churches unite together in the fullness of communion" (n. 30). This was a very hopeful way to phrase their message, since it assumes that full unity with the Orthodox will indeed become a reality. Several initiatives by Paul VI and John Paul II have drawn positive responses from the Orthodox side. This suggests that Vatican II's hopes were not ill-founded, although tensions still exist and flare up due to various exigencies.

Written when communist oppression was still a real phenomenon to be reckoned with, the decree ends on a note of solidarity as it invites all to pray for "the consolation of the Holy Spirit" on all those "many Christians, whatever church they belong to, who for their courageous profession of the name of Christ endure suffering and privation" (n. 30). This is a unity in prayer and tribulation that highlights the key fact that those issues dividing Orthodox and Catholics are of far less importance than the issues that unite them.

What is our unfinished agenda? Most Latin-rite Catholics still display a distressing ignorance of their Eastern-rite brothers and sisters. How exasperating it is to explain carefully that Eastern Catholics are truly full-fledged Catholics, only to have someone immediately label them as "Orthodox." This will only be remedied by personal study and appreciation for valid pluralism in the Church, which can best be gained by assisting at Eastern liturgies, when and where available.

Latin-rite Catholics in the United States can learn much from their Eastern brothers and sisters — most especially to recover our lost sense of the sacred, so magnificently expressed in the rich signs and symbols of the Eastern Churches. It would also be good to re-kindle a healthy love for tradition, something deeply ingrained in the Eastern consciousness. Finally, developing a taste for liturgical pluralism would be helpful, which will certainly be needed as newly received Anglicans maintain their own "usage" and the Tridentine rite co-exists with the reformed and normative liturgy of Vatican II.

Since the Council, some Eastern Catholics have developed a regrettable inferiority complex vis-à-vis the Orthodox. Abandoning slavish conformity to Roman ways, many now slavishly conform to Orthodoxy. In point of fact, Eastern Catholics have as much to teach their Orthodox brethren as they do to learn from them, precisely because of their experience of belonging to a Universal Church, of benefiting from a thousand-year theological development beyond 1054, and of living in communion with the Successor of Peter.

Two millennia of Christian "diversity in unity" display the Church's respect for all that is good in human culture. This also underscores our Faith's great strength, which not only survives but also thrives on such diversity. The Church does not want Easterners to become Latins or Latins to become Easterners. Instead, she wants us all to be faithful to our own traditions and thus build up the Body of Christ, which is composed of many different members under our one Head — Jesus Christ.

CHAPTER EIGHT

Redemptoris Missio
(Encyclical on the Permanent Validity of the Church's Missionary Mandate)

Address on Pope John Paul II's encyclical Redemptoris Missio, *for the inauguration of the Wojtyla Lecture Series in the Archdiocese of Denver, October 25, 1999.*

THE MOST IMPORTANT INSIGHT that can be gleaned from the teachings of the Second Vatican Council, in my estimation, is the universal call to holiness — that is, Our Lord's desire that every single one of us become a saint. Intimately connected to that is a line from St. Paul that informs us that God wants all men to be saved and to come to know the truth (cf. 1 Tm 2:4). And as St. Paul reminds the Romans, "And how are they to believe in him of whom they have never heard? And how are they to hear without a preacher? And how can men preach unless they are sent?" (Rom 10:14-15). In other words, salvation demands evangelization.

As I was preparing my reflections on this theme, I was struck by the fact that the relics of a young French cloistered nun were engaged in a worldwide tour and were just about to grace our nation with her holy presence. A cloistered nun on a worldwide tour! How odd, one might think, unless one knew something about that Religious.

In 1927, just thirty years after the death of St. Thérèse of Lisieux and two years after her canonization, Pope Pius XI named the Little Flower patroness of universal missions. Why? Let's allow the saint to tell us in her own words:

> I have the vocation of the Apostle. I would like to travel over the whole earth to preach your Name and to plant your glorious Cross on infidel soil. But, O my Beloved, one mission

alone would not be sufficient for me. I would want to preach the Gospel on all the five continents simultaneously and even to the most remote isles.

Interestingly, she had been considered by her community to help found new Carmels in Saigon and Hanoi, but when it became obvious that her health would not permit such ventures, she came to a deeper understanding of the missionary vocation. It was then that she concluded that her work of prayer was essential for the work of direct evangelization, at which point we hear her say to her sister Céline: "Is not the apostolate of prayer lifted higher, so to speak, than the apostolate of preaching? Our mission is to form those Gospel laborers. They will save millions of souls, whose mothers we shall be."

By a happy coincidence, just yesterday, the whole Church observed World Mission Sunday. Both facts call us to an examination of conscience: Do we Catholics living in this nation at the close of this century believe it our responsibility to see to it that all men worship the one true God revealed by Jesus Christ? Do we preach, in St. Paul's powerful phrase, "with full conviction" (1 Thess 1:5)?

Thirty years ago, the Fathers of the Second Vatican Council in their document on missionary activity, *Ad Gentes Divinitus*, spoke what they thought was a truism when they declared, "The Church on earth is by its very nature missionary" (n. 2). Much post-conciliar practice, however, would call that teaching into question, so much so that both Pope Paul VI in *Evangelii Nuntiandi* and Pope John Paul II in *Redemptoris Missio* would consider it their serious obligation to restate this basic truth of faith and to give new impetus to the Church's missionary work.

Permit me to serve as your guide today through *Redemptoris Missio*, so that together we may enter into the mind and heart of our Holy Father, to discover what he sees as the tasks confronting the Church on the brink of the third millennium. I am sure the issuance of this papal document in 1991 gladdened the heart of our mission-minded saint, and I suspect our review of it tonight would likewise be pleasing to her.

A synonym for missionary endeavor is *evangelization*, which simply means "spreading the Gospel." Although the number of Catholics has grown tremendously in the past three decades, we must shamefacedly admit that the number of full-time missionaries has declined precipitously; furthermore, the grand total of people who have never heard of Jesus Christ has actually doubled since the end of Vatican II. Why has this happened?

The Holy Father suggests several reasons, but two stand out among them all: first, a crisis of faith on the part of believing Christians, so that they have begun to question their own faith and are therefore uncomfortable or incapable of sharing it with others; second, a false sense of ecumenism that would mistakenly hold that respect for other Christians and other religions should silence our evangelistic mission. The Pope disagrees mightily and counters by reminding us that, in his words, "Faith is strengthened when it is given to others!" (n. 2). And even more to the point, the finest thing that anyone can do for another human being is to introduce that person to Jesus Christ.

This massive papal document — 150 pages in length — seeks to accomplish many other goals as well: to clear up confusion about the necessity of witnessing to unbelievers; to encourage missionaries in their important work; to foster vocations among clergy, Religious, and laity for mission lands; to stimulate theologians to teach and write more on the meaning of evangelization; to persuade dioceses to send out missionaries and to commit their resources to such projects; and to assure non-Christian nations that the Church's only purpose in evangelization is to share Christ — not to dominate or impose alien political or social norms.

Pope John Paul sees the present moment as particularly suited to this critical effort, especially due to advances in communications and travel, but also because modern man seems to be more attuned to so many of the values taught by Our Lord: a desire for peace, a concern for the needy, and a thirst for social justice. Beyond that, the more man becomes overwhelmed by technology, the more he usually searches for spiritual consolation. The time is ripe then — or is it? First, it is crucial to tackle some of the questions that have been raised about either the importance or the validity of missionary activity.

Is converting people to Jesus Christ still relevant? The Pope pointedly asks: "Has it not been replaced by interreligious dialogue? Is not human development an adequate goal for the Church's mission?" (n. 4). Doesn't preaching violate freedom and conscience? Can't human beings be saved in any religion? I'm sure you've heard people make such statements, perhaps missionaries themselves and even in their own magazines. But the New Testament resounds with a contrary answer, as Jesus asserts: "No one comes to the Father, but by me" (Jn 14:6). And the apostles after Him declare, "There is no other name under heaven given among men by which we must be saved" (Acts 4:12). So, let's take these questions and try to answer them, one by one.

Dialogue is good and wholesome, but it is not an end in itself. Dialogue helps to clear away misconceptions; it aids us in expressing our respect for others; it provides friendly terrain on which to communicate as fellow human beings, created in the image and likeness of the one true God. Nevertheless, the Holy Father warns us: "Dialogue should be implemented and conducted with the conviction that the Church is the ordinary means of salvation and that she alone possesses the fullness of the means of salvation" (n. 55).

What about human development as a worthwhile expression of evangelization? It, too, is good but inadequate. Providing for the needs of the hungry, the naked, the homeless, and the ignorant are holy things to do. In truth, Jesus tells us that we shall be judged at the end of time on how well we did such things (cf. Mt 25:40), but that same Jesus also taught Satan that "man shall not live by bread alone." On what else does he live? "By every word that proceeds from the mouth of God" (Mt 4:4). So, yes, it is our Christian responsibility to care for men's bodies — but even more so for their souls.

Does missionary work violate human freedom and dignity? We must sadly admit that at times missionaries did conduct themselves in inappropriate ways in certain places, but the Church herself never sanctioned such methods. Coming to Christ is possible only when the human person is fully respected, which is to say that the preacher must never forget that every human being has the inestimable gifts of intellect and free will — and only when those are touched can a person make a decision for or against Christ. Presenting the truth in love is the most powerful sign of respect for freedom and dignity, at one and the same time.

Finally, what about this notion of people being saved in any religion? Certainly, it is true that salvation can occur outside the visible boundaries of the Catholic Church. *Redemptoris Missio* notes that well: "The universality of salvation means that it is granted not only to those who explicitly believe in Christ and have entered the Church" (n. 10). But the Church and her sacraments are indeed the *normal* means of salvation, and just as importantly, it is our privilege and obligation to see to it that as many of God's children learn that truth as possible. In other words, I always say that I am not so concerned about what God will do with millions of unbaptized Chinese as I am about what He will do with *me* because countless millions have not heard about His divine Son.

Which leads logically to our personal involvement and commitment to evangelization. Our tasks are many as committed Catholics who, for the most part, will never venture beyond our borders to preach the Gospel. What can — and should — we do?

First of all, we must enfold the Church's missionary activity in our daily prayer. Although the Lord has not called us to be missionaries in the strict sense of the word, He does expect us to be missionary cooperators. St. Thérèse always wanted to be a missionary, but her weak health did not allow for it. Instead, the Little Flower gradually realized that she could be a missionary by uniting herself in prayer to the sacrifices of those in the foreign missions. The support of our prayers is critical for the success of the contemporary work of evangelization.

Secondly, a devout Catholic will support the missions financially. This is another way of being a part of the overall effort to preach the Gospel to all creation. Such gifts ought to be generous and sacrificial in nature, never stingy or token. At the same time, you must be sure that your contributions are going to worthy missionary associations, faithful to Christ and to the teaching authority of the Church. That is why gifts to well-known organizations like the Society for the Propagation of the Faith, the Holy Childhood Association, or the Catholic Near East Welfare Association are always "safe bets."

Thirdly, we need to take yet another cue from the patroness of the Church's missions. As she suffered almost unbearable pain and a most agonizing death, St. Thérèse determined not to allow that suffering to "go to waste." On the contrary, she insisted on putting to good use her depressions, her doubts, her confusion, and her near-despair. How? By joining her sufferings to those of the Suffering Christ, thereby making them meritorious — and one of the intentions uppermost in her mind was the saving of souls. How much human suffering, however, does "go to waste," either because it is resisted, or resented, or just passively endured. The headache; the anxiety over an impending medical examination; the depression that comes from loneliness, old age, or being misunderstood — all of these are sufferings that can be "offered up" for holy intentions like the salvation of the world.

Fourthly, become an informed Catholic. Read and reread the documents of the Second Vatican Council, especially texts like those on missionary activity and the role of the laity in the world. Study Sacred Scripture; become completely familiar with the *Catechism of the Catholic Church*. Subscribe to good Catholic literature, which presents the Catholic Faith in all its truth and in total fidelity to the teachings of the Holy Father. St. Thérèse knew this well; hence, in her "Last Conversations," we hear her say: "I can nourish myself on nothing but the truth." This sounds like an echo of the Divine Teacher Himself, Who declared, "My food is to do the will of him who sent me, and to accomplish his work" (Jn 4:34). Or yet again, there is His holy counsel: "Do not labor for the food which perishes, but for the food which endures to eternal life" (Jn 6:27).

Fifthly, you must be a witness to the Gospel in the circumstances of your own life. Most of Europe and the Americas are lands where the Gospel once flowered so beautifully; today, that is no longer the case, unfortunately. The Holy Father said this in *Tertio Millennio Adveniente*, no doubt with a great degree of sadness. He wrote, "The more the West is becoming estranged from its Christian roots, the more it is becoming missionary territory" (n. 57). The Pope calls this type of preaching "re-evangelization" or "the new evangelization." God has placed us in a time and place where that is the work most urgent to perform — and we cannot exempt ourselves from it. Get involved in the Legion of Mary or an apologetics group committed to explaining and defending our holy Faith. That also means creating a climate of faith, so that you can impart the saving message of Christ and His Church at home to relatives who have lost their way, at work, at school, in the neighborhood, in the marketplace — wherever the Gospel light no longer shines, or does so only dimly. In the contemporary darkness, you are to be bearers of the light of Christ, whether convenient or inconvenient (cf. 2 Tm 4:2). St. Francis of Assisi counseled his brethren: "Always preach; sometimes use words." Or as Pope Paul VI put it so well: "Modern man listens more willingly to witnesses than to teachers, and if he does listen to teachers, it is because they are witnesses" (*Evangelii Nuntiandi*, n. 41).

Sixthly, we need to ask ourselves how well people — even in our nominally Christian culture — have heard and understood the message of Christ and His Church. We must examine our consciences to determine if occasions of our bad example or of our poor communication of Christ's truth have been obstacles to a proper hearing for the Gospel. In other words, have some people really rejected Christ or His Gospel — or merely rejected our faulty presentation of either? Obviously, this is what Msgr. Ronald Knox had in mind when he said: "There is no single excuse so freely used by people who want to justify themselves in remaining outside the Church as the behaviour of some of us who are inside it."[56]

Finally, allow me to offer a very practical, verifiable application of what I have been saying — a suggestion in two parts. In the next twelve months, make it your goal to bring into the fullness of life and love that is found in the Catholic Church one person not presently visibly joined to her; in that same time period, make it your goal to bring back one person who, for whatever reason, has left the Church or distanced himself from her.

St. Teresa of Ávila implored her nuns to consider as their "business matters" (to use her terminology) the support in prayer of defenders of the Faith and missionaries. The Little Flower had integrated that admonition into the very fabric of her spirituality. Hence, we hear her say: "The cry of Jesus on the Cross sounded continually in my heart: 'I thirst!' These words ignited within me an unknown and very living fire. I wanted to give my Beloved to drink, and I felt myself consumed with a thirst for souls." Does that same spirit inflame you? It should.

The Mass of the Roman rite ends with the stark dismissal: *"Ite, missa est."* What does that mean? Literally, "Go, it has been sent." What has been sent? The Church. To do what? To proclaim the Gospel. Simply stated, the Eucharist, the Church, and evangelization are intimately connected to one another — indeed, they are inseparable. And so it is that the work for which each celebration of the Eucharistic Sacrifice prepares us is precisely that of spreading the Gospel; it is the work to which we must recommit ourselves and for which we seek the powerful intercession of St. Thérèse, patroness of the universal missions.

CHAPTER NINE

⌖

Ut Unum Sint
(Encyclical on Commitment to Ecumenism)

SEVERAL OBSERVERS OF POPE JOHN PAUL II'S pontificate have suggested that one can gain a clue to his vision for the Church of the final years of the second millennium by considering his encyclicals, with the first phase centering on the internal life of the Catholic Church and the second phase on the ways the Church interacts with the world-at-large. *Ut Unum Sint,* promulgated in 1995, falls into the latter category at first blush but also participates in the former category. Yes, it would seem that relations between the Catholic Church and other Christian communities is an example of *ad extra* concerns; however, inasmuch as unity is a hallmark of the Church, it is equally an *ad intra* affair. The encyclical, like ancient Gaul, is divided into three parts: the Catholic Church's commitment to ecumenism; the fruits of dialogue; and the road ahead.

The Pope launches into his topic by establishing a connection between Christian unity and the impending Great Jubilee of the Year 2000, even as he lifts up for veneration the memory of the millions of martyrs who gave their lives for Christ in the century just about to close — including martyrs representing "Churches and Ecclesial Communities not in full communion with the Catholic Church" (n. 1). In some sense, the need to celebrate the two-thousandth anniversary of the Incarnation *together* as Christians and the suffering *together* for the cause of Christ provide an apt framework for reflection on the Lord's desire that His disciples be one.

The Holy Father acknowledges that the path to reunion has been "difficult," but that the "positive and tangible results . . . [encourage] us to move forward." Nor does he "sugarcoat" the situation. The obstacles are not merely theological; they are attitudinal, rooted in "misunderstandings and prejudices." "Complacency, indifference and insufficient knowledge of one another often make the situation worse," thus demanding a "necessary purification of past memories." This can be done best, he maintains, when Christians commit themselves "to re-examine together their painful past" (n. 2)

Lest other Christians think he is speaking in superficial terms, John Paul declares emphatically that "at the Second Vatican Council, the Catholic Church committed herself *irrevocably* to following the path of the ecumenical venture" (n. 3; emphasis in the original). In other words, from the Catholic point of view, there is no turning back.

Furthermore, the Church does not hesitate to "confess the weaknesses of her members, conscious that their sins are so many betrayals and obstacles to the accomplishment of the Savior's plan."[57] He expresses the hope that the new millennium "will be an exceptional occasion" to advance the cause of Christian unity. Indeed, as the first millennium was a time of relative ecclesial unity and the second millennium a period of one tragic schism after another, the third millennium might see a return to unity. To that end, the Pontiff says, "I myself intend to promote every suitable initiative," particularly since the unity of the Church "is a specific duty of the Bishop of Rome as the Successor of the Apostle Peter" (nn. 3-4).

With the stage set, the Pope then moves into an analysis of "the Catholic Church's commitment to ecumenism," rehearsing all the familiar texts of Sacred Scripture that suggest themselves, from the Prophet Ezekiel to the Gospel according to St. John. Affirming the teaching of Vatican II, found especially in *Lumen Gentium* and *Unitatis Redintegratio,* he asserts that the Church "embraces with hope the commitment to ecumenism as a duty of the Christian conscience enlightened by faith and guided by love" (n. 8). With a striking firmness, he says that "God wills the Church, because he wills unity" (n. 9). Thus, the Church is the very instrument chosen by God from all eternity to bring about the unity of the human family. And this is the case because the communion of the members of the Church is to be a reflection of the communion among the members of the Blessed Trinity, in Whose life all the baptized share.

Ever faithful to the truth and refusing to water down the truth for the sake of a pseudo-unity, the Holy Father repeats the clear doctrine of Vatican II — namely, that the Church of Christ "subsists in the Catholic Church," even while recognizing that "many elements of sanctification and of truth can be found outside her visible structure." The Council Fathers went on to stress that these very "elements" provide the impetus or "inner dynamism towards Catholic unity" (n. 10). While rejoicing in the Catholic Church's preservation in unity and the fullness of truth, the Pope admits, echoing Vatican II, that in the shameful divisions that have marred the visage of Christ's Bride, "people of both sides were to blame" (n. 11).

Rather than dwelling on the negative, we are led to recall: that because of our common Baptism, all Christians have a real, even if imperfect, communion with the Catholic Church; that "elements of sanctification and truth" (n. 11) work in various ways outside the visible boundaries of the Catholic Church; and that particular attention must be paid to the Orthodox Churches because of their maintenance of the episcopate and, hence, the Eucharist. The aim, then, is to recognize the unity that already exists and to direct energies "to making the partial communion existing between Christians grow towards full communion in truth and charity" (n. 14). For this to occur, however, personal and communal conversion are called for, especially "an increased sense of the need for repentance" (n. 15). This awareness must impress itself on the consciousness of individuals and communities alike: "No Christian community can exempt itself from this call" (n. 16).

Equally important is an adherence to doctrine, without which true unity is impossible; at the same time, "doctrine needs to be presented in a way that makes it understandable to those for whom God intended it" (n. 18). Doctrinal compromise is not honest, for it creates an illusion of unity. Or as John Paul astutely notes, "In matters of faith, compromise is in contradiction with God who is Truth" (n. 18). However, as Blessed John XXIII pointed out at the opening of Vatican II, the Deposit of Faith is one thing, and the way it is explained is another. In other words, a new time and new place may call for new methods and new explanations, which is very different from a denial or repudiation of doctrine.

To this moment, it may appear that the entire program of ecumenism is predicated on carefully concocted schemes and plans; nothing could be further from the truth. Therefore, we read about the centrality of prayer. As St. Ignatius of Loyola was fond of teaching, in any endeavor we ought to work so hard as to suggest that everything depends upon us and to pray so hard as to suggest that everything depends upon Almighty God; this is the winning formula. Beyond that, prayer in common is a powerful testimony to the unity that already exists and is a yet more powerful stimulus to grow in the unity of faith and love. Not surprisingly, we hear the Pope remind us that "this love finds its most complete expression in common prayer" (n. 21). More to the point, "when Christians pray together, the goal of unity seems closer" (n. 22), and "fellowship in prayer leads people to look at the Church and Christianity in a new way" (n. 23).

In discussing prayer in common, the Holy Father highlights the importance of the Week of Prayer for Christian Unity. He likewise identifies various occasions in his pontificate when prayer in common with other Christians was particularly poignant, including encounters with the Primate of the Anglican Communion, as well as with other Christian leaders in Scandinavia, North and South America, Africa, and at the headquarters of the World Council of Churches. Lifted up for special consideration is the service in St. Peter's Basilica during which he and Patriarch Dimitrios I "recited together the Nicene-Constantinopolitan Creed according to its original Greek text" (n. 24).[58]

Following upon prayer is dialogue, which the Pope says "is rooted in the nature of the person and his dignity" (n. 28). Here, the "personalist" philosopher in him comes to the fore, as he expounds on how dialogue expresses concretely man's "sincere gift of himself." This is not just "talk" for its own sake but a true "exchange of gifts" (n. 28). Furthermore, dialogue demands "reciprocity," viewing the other not as an object but as "a partner." He goes on to write, "When undertaking dialogue, each side must presuppose in the other a desire for reconciliation, for unity in truth" (n. 29). Interestingly, he sees a connection between dialogue and examination of conscience. Dialogue, however, is not just between two human parties; it necessarily involves Almighty God and, in fact, has "a primarily vertical thrust, directed towards the One who, as the Redeemer of the world and the Lord of history, is himself our Reconciliation" (n. 35).

At the horizontal level, though, "dialogue is also a natural instrument for comparing differing points of view and, above all, for examining those disagreements which hinder full communion between Christians." Lest anyone suppose that this conversation is little more than "whispering sweet nothings," the Pontiff makes clear that "love for the truth is the deepest dimension of any authentic quest for full communion between Christians" (n. 36). Also necessary are the virtues of charity and humility, whereby one is open to the other and equally open to the fullness of truth. In this context, it is essential to remember that "the whole body of doctrine [must] be clearly presented" and that it is important to explain the truth "in a way that is correct, fair and understandable." But there is more: "At the same time [it must take] into account both the way of thinking and the actual historical experiences of the other party." And then the point is driven home one more time: "Full communion of course will have to come about through the acceptance of the whole truth" and "facile 'agreement' must be absolutely avoided" (n. 36).

The Holy Father offers as an example of authentic dialogue the resolution of Christological conflicts with the ancient Churches of the East, in which the goal was "to determine whether the words involved say the same thing." The conclusion was that they did. And so, whereas for centuries, "intolerant polemics and controversies have made incompatible assertions out of what was really the result of two different ways of looking at the same reality," true dialogue was able to determine the underlying truth held in common by both sides (n. 38).

Then the realist in the Pope comes out, as he does not hesitate to acknowledge that "real and genuine disagreements in matters of faith" do exist and that these "should be faced in a spirit of fraternal charity, of respect for the demands of one's own conscience and of the conscience of the other party, with profound humility and love for the truth." He does not hesitate to assert that Catholics have an "ace in the hole," since they have the "living Magisterium" to assist them in apprehending the truth (n. 39).

Finally, the Holy Father calls for "practical cooperation." Simply put, ecumenism is not just something "spiritual" or an academic exercise; prayer, study, and dialogue need to issue forth in common action "at all levels: pastoral, cultural and social, as well as that of witnessing to the Gospel message." He argues that "ecumenical cooperation is a true school of ecumenism," as believers come to know one another better as they serve the world together. And not to be dismissed lightly, "in the eyes of the world, cooperation among Christians becomes a form of common Christian witness and a means of evangelization which benefits all involved" (n. 40).

When a commitment to ecumenism is in place, what can one expect to see? Chapter II offers a picture that is quite appealing: brotherhood rediscovered; solidarity in the service of humanity; approaching one another through the Word of God and through divine worship;[59] and appreciating the endowments present among other Christians.[60] John Paul singles out "growth in communion" as *the* concrete sign of the success of the ecumenical movement; here he identifies the many "bilateral theological dialogues" (n. 49), especially those with the Churches of the East, as well as "resuming contacts"[61] and mutual recognition by Catholics and Orthodox of one another as "sister Churches" (n. 52).[62] He likewise appeals to the Eastern Catholic Churches to "play a constructive role in the dialogue of love and in the theological dialogue at both the local and international levels, and thus contribute to mutual understanding and the continuing pursuit of full unity" (n. 60).

In a similar vein, the Pope speaks of "the Ancient Churches of the East" — that is, those "which rejected the dogmatic formulations of the Councils of Ephesus and Chalcedon," predating by centuries the 1054 split between East and West. With great satisfaction, he shows how the contacts of both Pope Paul VI and himself with the bishops of these bodies have advanced the ecumenical agenda, particularly the "common Christological declaration" he signed with the Assyrian Patriarch of the East, Mar Dinkha IV in 1994 (n. 62).

Moving on to "dialogue with other Churches and Ecclesial Communities in the West," the Pope situates the present state of affairs in a context "of an historical and psychological nature, and the other theological and doctrinal" (n. 64). Not to be overlooked is that differences not only exist between the Catholic Church and the several ecclesial communities harking back to the Reformation, but among these communities themselves — an aspect of the question often overlooked but one that adds an additional and important dimension to the work of Christian unity. The Holy Father praises the efforts of the World Council of Churches, noting with approval Catholic membership in the Commission on Faith and Order.

He goes on to review some of the high points of contact between the post-conciliar popes and many Protestant bodies. With obvious emotion and tenderness, John Paul cites an event in 1991 when he was the celebrant of the canonization Mass for Bridget of Sweden, and the Lutheran bishops in attendance approached him at Communion time for his blessing, repeating this gesture that they had performed during a papal visit to the Scandinavian and Nordic countries. He also refers to the famous 1986 Assisi World Day of Prayer for Peace, which included not only Christians but also Jews and other non-Christians. One senses a feeling of satisfaction and accomplishment in the Pope's tone as he ends this section of the encyclical.

Chapter III has a Latin title, *"Quanta est nobis via?"* ("How much further have we to go?"). Once again, very realistically, John Paul sums it up thus:

> The ultimate goal of the ecumenical movement is to re-establish full visible unity among all the baptized. In view of this goal, all the results so far attained are but one stage of the journey, however promising and positive [n. 77].

In other words, we have a long way to go. This will "require patient and courageous efforts." He adds: "In this process, one must not impose any burden beyond that which is strictly necessary" (n. 78), alluding to Acts 15:28.

He then lays out a concrete program, identifying five "areas in need of fuller study": the relationship between Scripture and Tradition; the Eucharist, especially in regard to its sacrificial dimension and the Real Presence; Holy Orders understood as a sacrament; the authority of the Magisterium; and the intercessory role of the Blessed Virgin Mary as "Mother of God and Icon of the Church." "In this courageous journey towards unity," he says, "the transparency and the prudence of faith require us to avoid both false irenicism and indifference to the Church's ordinances" (n. 79).

But there is more: "Conversely, that same transparency and prudence urge us to reject a halfhearted commitment to unity and, even more, a prejudicial opposition or a defeatism which tends to see everything in negative terms." Having to "take account of all the demands of revealed truth" is the first condition for the journey, but that "does not mean to put a brake on the ecumenical movement." "On the contrary," he warns, "it means preventing it from settling for apparent solutions which would lead to no firm and solid results" (n. 79).

Nor does he evince a kind of "Pollyannaish" approach to all this; in truth, he is extremely demanding and even hard-nosed: "For the outcome of dialogue to be received [that is, becoming "a common heritage"], there is needed a broad and precise critical process which analyzes the results and rigorously tests their consistency with the Tradition of faith received from the Apostles and lived out in the community of believers gathered around the Bishop, their legitimate Pastor" (n. 80). When the time is ripe, "the Church's teaching authority is responsible for expressing a definitive judgment" (n. 81).

Meanwhile, it remains for all Christians — not just pastors or theologians — to make their personal contribution to Christian unity by engaging in spiritual ecumenism and by bearing witness to holiness in their own lives. With no hesitation, the Pope indicates that the Church of Rome has a unique contribution to make in and through the Petrine office, which "has now become a subject of study" across the board. "After centuries of bitter controversies," he observes, "the other Churches and Ecclesial Communities are more and more taking a fresh look at this ministry of unity" (n. 89).

He then stakes out the theological foundations for this office over several pages but also concludes thus: "I insistently pray the Holy Spirit to shine His light upon us, enlightening all the Pastors and theologians of our Churches, that we may seek — together, of course — the forms in which this ministry may accomplish a service of love recognized by all concerned" (n. 95). This is an immense challenge, but one that has been well received by many of the partners in the dialogue.

Chapter III ends by linking Christian unity to "the glory of the Father" (n. 98) and for effective evangelization.

The entire encyclical is summed up in a brief but powerful exhortation. The Holy Father calls on his brother-bishops in the Catholic Church to imitate him in making ecumenism a pastoral priority, in fidelity to the Second Vatican Council. He asks that the Church receive the grace of the Holy Spirit "to strengthen her own unity and to make it grow towards full communion with other Christians" (n. 102).

"How is the Church to obtain this grace?" he asks. "In the first place, through prayer." Secondly, "through giving thanks." Thirdly, "through hope in the Spirit." "And should we ask if all this is possible, the answer will always be yes. It is the same answer which Mary of Nazareth heard: with God nothing is impossible." Citing St. Cyprian, John Paul gives a practical motivation for a commitment to Christian unity: "God does not accept the sacrifice of a sower of disunion" (n. 102).

His final plea is presented as a rhetorical question: "At the dawn of the new millennium, how can we not implore from the Lord, with renewed enthusiasm and a deeper awareness, the grace to prepare ourselves, together, to offer this sacrifice of unity?" (n. 102). The pontificate of Pope John Paul II has been a prolonged response to that question, which he obviously hopes becomes the question that preoccupies every baptized Christian.

CHAPTER TEN

≈

Orientale Lumen
(Apostolic Letter on the Eastern Churches)

THE DOCUMENT CURRENTLY UNDER CONSIDERATION is not an encyclical but an apostolic letter; although of lesser theological weight than the former, it nonetheless is an important teaching tool of the Sovereign Pontiff. *Orientale Lumen* ("The Light of the East") was written by Pope John Paul II in 1995 to commemorate the centennial of Pope Leo XIII's promulgation of his apostolic letter *Orientalium Dignitas*, dealing with "the significance of the Eastern traditions for the whole Church" (n. 1). The issuance of this letter also appeared thirty years after the conclusion of the Second Vatican Council, with its decree on the Eastern Churches.

"The Pope, son of a Slav people" (n. 3), sees it as particularly appropriate that he assist the whole Church in coming to a deeper appreciation of her Eastern heritage; he goes so far as to say that this is necessary for "the full manifestation of the Church's catholicity" (n. 1). But this interest is not unique to John Paul II; he is actually at pains to demonstrate that his concern is in line with that of "many other Popes in the past," especially as that relates to the question of the unity between the Churches of East and West. This is most pressing because "we have almost everything in common; and above all, we have in common the true longing for unity" (n. 3).

The first section of the letter is titled "Knowing the Christian East — An Experience of Faith." The old Baltimore Catechism informed us that our goal in life was to "know, love, and serve God." The order of the verbs was not accidental; knowledge precedes love and service in any relationship, and that is what the Holy Father is suggesting here. He humbly admits that in the course of history, "sometimes one tradition has come nearer to a full appreciation of some aspects of a mystery of revelation than the other." These alternative formulations, however, ought to be perceived as "complementary rather than conflicting" (n. 5).

With equal humility, he declares: "I do not intend to describe [the Eastern] heritage or to interpret it: I listen to the Churches of the East, which I know are living interpreters of the treasure of tradition they preserve" (n. 5). This is a fundamental key to ecumenical dialogue — the willingness to take seriously the other as a person with dignity and to enter into his experience.

The Pope selects several qualities that seem to characterize Eastern Christianity. The first and most obvious is its devotion to the Sacred Liturgy. The second flows from the first: an emphasis on *theosis*, or divinization — that is, "participation in the divine nature through communion with the mystery of the Holy Trinity." Eastern theology is most attentive to the special role played by the Holy Spirit in the life of the Church, in the individual Christian, and in the whole of creation transformed in and through the Incarnation. The Virgin Mary as "an icon of the Church" is most important in Eastern Christian theology and spirituality (n. 6). Although these Churches emphasize the indwelling of the Triune God in the hearts of believers, particularly in the sacraments, there is an equally strong tendency to stand in awe and wonder before these realities. Finally, one cannot think of the East without immediately thinking of monasticism, which arose there and then was introduced to the West.

Starting with Sts. Cyril and Methodius, a hallmark of the Church of the East has always been "the attention given to peoples and their cultures." Citing his own encyclical on these two apostles to the Slavs, the Holy Father asserts: "By incarnating the Gospel in the native culture of the peoples which they were evangelizing, Saints Cyril and Methodius were especially meritorious for the formation and development of that same culture, or rather of many cultures." He continues: "They combined respect and consideration for individual cultures with a passion for the universality of the Church, which they tirelessly strove to achieve" (n. 7). He terms this "an authoritative example of successful inculturation," which teaches us "that if we wish to avoid the recurrence of particularism as well as of exaggerated nationalism, we must realize that the proclamation of the Gospel should be deeply rooted in what is distinctive to each culture and open to convergence in a universality, which involves an exchange for the sake of mutual enrichment" (n. 7).

Another gift of Eastern Christianity, according to the Pope, is its reverence for Tradition, coupled with a lively eschatological expectation. Tradition, however, should not be mistaken for intransigence, and he has this warning: "When the uses and customs belonging to each Church are considered as absolutely unchangeable, there is a sure risk of Tradition losing that feature of a living reality which grows and develops, and which the Spirit guarantees precisely because it has something to say to the people of every age." Furthermore, "Tradition is never pure nostalgia for things or forms past, nor regret for lost privileges, but the living memory of the Bride, kept eternally youthful by the Love that dwells within her." He also cautions that "each Church must struggle against the temptation to make an absolute of what it does." Tradition is balanced by expectation, which "urges [the Churches] to be what they have not yet fully become" (n. 8).

In a rather novel fashion, the Holy Father indicates his desire "to look at the vast panorama of Eastern Christianity from a specific vantage point which affords a view of many of its features," and he selects monasticism, to which he refers as "a model of baptismal life" and "a symbolic synthesis of Christianity." John Paul says, without fear of contradiction, that "monasticism has always been the very soul of the Eastern Churches" (n. 9).[63]

"Monasticism shows in a special way," he writes, "that life is suspended between two poles: the Word of God and the Eucharist." For the monk, the Word of God is the point of departure, listening to which changes his life. This Word is heard in meditative personal reading, in the Divine Office, and in the Eastern hymnody (which is intensely biblical). "The Eucharist is the culmination of this prayer experience, the other pole indissolubly bound to the Word, as the place where the Word becomes Flesh and Blood, a heavenly experience where this becomes an event" (n. 10).

The Holy Father speaks of the Eastern perception of worship as "a liturgy for the whole man and for the whole cosmos." He explains:

> Within this framework, liturgical prayer in the East shows a great aptitude for involving the human person in his or her totality: the mystery is sung in the loftiness of its content, but also in the warmth of the sentiments it awakens in the heart of redeemed humanity. In the sacred act, even bodiliness is summoned to praise, and beauty, which in the East is one of the best loved names expressing the divine harmony and the model of humanity transfigured, appears everywhere: in the shape of the church, in the sounds, in the colors, in the lights, in the scents. The lengthy duration of the celebrations, the repeated invocations, everything expresses gradual identification with the mystery celebrated with one's whole person. Thus the prayer of the Church already becomes participation in the heavenly liturgy, an anticipation of the final beatitude [n. 11].

This is surely fulsome praise as the Pope rhapsodizes on how the Eastern Churches harness all of creation to laud and magnify the Creator. This approach is possible, however, because — as he reminds us — "Christianity does not reject matter" but sees the bodily, the physical, the earthly, brought into "the process of transfiguration, pneumatization [being enlivened by the Spirit]," a kind of foretaste of "recapitulation in Christ the Lord" of all creation in the eschaton (n. 11).

The Holy Father also regards monasticism as offering "a clear look at self-discovery." In a lovely turn of phrase, he writes: "The monk turns his gaze to Christ, God and man. In the disfigured face of Christ, the man of sorrow, he sees the prophetic announcement of the transfigured face of the Risen Christ." He explains that "this gaze progressively conformed to Christ thus learns detachment from externals, from the tumult of the senses, from all that keeps man from that freedom which allows him to be grasped by the Spirit" (n. 12). Once more, the monk is presented as a paradigm of Christian existence.

Moving ahead, we learn that "a monk's way is not generally marked by personal effort alone" (n. 13), as a spiritual father tailors the journey into God; we are not "lone rangers." This notion of communion is essential to grasp as "monasticism shows us how there is no true vocation that is not born of the Church and for the Church." John Paul sees a particular gift of Eastern monastic communion as having "always been careful to guarantee the superiority of love over every law." The Pope writes, "This communion is revealed first and foremost in service to one's brothers in monastic life, but also to the Church community, in forms which vary in time and place, ranging from social assistance to itinerant preaching." He identifies evangelization as one of the most positive examples of communion become service: "Indeed it can be said that monasticism in antiquity — and at various time in subsequent ages too — has been the privileged means for the evangelization of peoples" (n. 14).

The Pope views the monk as "a person in relationship," so that "knowledge and participation are thus a single reality." This happens, in a preeminent manner, through the mystery of the Incarnation and God's desire that man become "the icon of the Icon" (n. 15). Even though we participate in this wondrous mystery, it is nonetheless "enveloped in silence." We can never penetrate this reality in its totality, and "thus is born what is called the apophatism[64] of the Christian East: the more man grows in the knowledge of God, the more he perceives him as an inaccessible mystery, whose essence cannot be grasped." The Pope cautions, "This should not be confused with an obscure mysticism in which man loses himself in enigmatic, impersonal realities." Unlike Buddhism, for instance, "the culmination of the knowledge and experience of God . . . is reached through prayerful assimilation of scripture and the liturgy more than by systematic meditation" (n. 16).

So, these are the facts that the Pontiff thinks Western Christians ought to apprehend about Eastern Christianity. And so, in the letter's second section, we are led "from knowledge to encounter," as he endeavors to join head to heart, so as to engage the whole person. He brings into clear relief many meetings he has had with Eastern leaders as sources of deep joy and satisfaction, but he highlights one very different type of encounter: "Sometimes urgent appeals from other Churches threatened or stricken with violence and abuse have reached this See of Rome. It has sought to open its heart to them all" (n. 17). This is another example of communion become service.

In a somewhat wistful fashion, John Paul declares: "Every day, I have a growing desire to go over the history of the Churches, in order to write at last a history of our unity and thus return to the time when, after the Death and Resurrection of the Lord Jesus, the Gospel spread to the most varied cultures and a most fruitful exchange began which still today is evidenced in the liturgies of the Churches." In his rehearsal of history, he is quick to point out that "the first councils are an eloquent witness to this enduring unity in diversity" (n. 18).

While acknowledging that dogmatic misunderstandings and conflicts existed in the first centuries (often, he observes, "magnified by the influence of political and cultural factors"), "we cannot forget that unity between Rome and Constantinople endured for the whole of the first millennium, despite difficulties." And even in the second millennium, when estrangement became a sad fact of life, "constructive meetings between Church leaders desirous of intensifying relations and fostering exchanges did not cease, nor did the holy efforts of men and women who, recognizing the setting of one group against the other as a grave sin, and being in love with unity and charity, attempted in many ways to promote the search for communion by prayer, study and reflection, and by open and cordial interaction" (n. 18).

Writing shortly after the fall of communism, the Holy Father observes that it would be sad that those "who together had suffered persecution" would now begin to "regard one another with suspicion and fear just when prospects and hopes of greater freedom are appearing." He strikingly calls this "a new, serious risk of sin which we must all make every effort to overcome." He places before the

Christians of Eastern Europe a stark set of options: "Today we can cooperate in proclaiming the Kingdom or we can become the upholders of new divisions." He then asks, "How can we be fully credible if we stand divided before the Eucharist, if we cannot live our sharing in the same Lord whom we are called to proclaim to the world?" (n. 19). Regrettably, his warning has gone largely unheeded.

John Paul proceeds to tackle another difficult issue. "Claiming that the whole array of uses and customs of the Latin Church is more complete or better suited to showing the fullness of correct doctrine" is unjustified. What is needed on the part of all is the contribution of "sensitivity and creativity," born of love (n. 20). The Pope also hints that this creativity may have to extend to theological and canonical categories to bring about the desired unity.

As for the Eastern Churches in full communion with Rome, he urges: "And if sometimes, in their relations with the Orthodox Churches, misunderstandings and open opposition have arisen, we all know that we must ceaselessly implore divine mercy and a new heart capable of reconciliation over and above any wrong suffered or inflicted" (n. 21).

Now John Paul is ready to proffer a program of common action. The first element he discusses has to do with the emergence of various Orthodox Churches from their catacomb-like existence and the need they have for assistance; he gladly puts the communities of the West at their disposal. In fact, Aid to the Church in Need, an international Catholic charity organization, took this papal challenge to heart and has been rendering support as needed to Orthodox and Catholic communities alike. Beyond this, the Pope gives a detailed picture of what is involved for the Christians of the West:

> . . . to know the liturgy of the Eastern Churches; to deepen their knowledge of the spiritual traditions of the Fathers and Doctors of the Christian East; to follow the example of the Eastern Churches for the inculturation of the Gospel message; to combat tensions between Latins and Orientals and to encourage dialogue between Catholics and the Orthodox; to

train in specialized institutions theologians, liturgists, historians and canonists for the Christian East, who in turn can spread knowledge of the Eastern Churches; to offer appropriate teaching on these subjects in seminaries and theological faculties, especially to future priests [n. 24].

He concludes this "laundry list" of agenda items with this stunning remark: "These remain very sound recommendations on which I intend to *insist* with particular force" (n. 24; emphasis added).

The Holy Father also calls on Catholic monasteries and pontifical universities "to extend this welcome on a wider scale" and for the founding of places of "hospitality to our brothers of the East, including such places in this city of Rome" (n. 25). Without being petulant, one could rightly ask if one can expect this kind of openness from the other side, but the Pope does seem to be holding Catholics to a higher standard. He likewise urges inter-parish activities and joint pilgrimages as fruitful opportunities for encounter.

Interestingly, the Pontiff sees the pluralistic countries of the West as unique experiments in fostering Christian unity. In looking at various diaspora communities, he has several suggestions: that Latin ordinaries faithfully observe the laws and principles of ecumenical cooperation and also see to the "pastoral care of the faithful of the Eastern Catholic Churches, especially when they lack their own hierarchy"; that Eastern Catholic bishops and clergy "collaborate closely with the Latin Ordinaries for an effective apostolate which is not fragmented"; that where Eastern clergy are not available, Latin clergy take care of the spiritual needs of the Eastern brethren, even while seeing "that those faithful grow in the awareness and knowledge of their own tradition" (n. 26).

This, then, is the pastoral plan and summary of the aspirations of Pope John Paul II in regard to Eastern Christianity. He concludes the document with this touching prayer:

> May God shorten the time and distance [of the journey toward full ecclesial communion]. May Christ, the *Orientale*

Lumen, soon, very soon, grant us to discover that in fact, despite so many centuries of distance, we were very close, because together — perhaps without knowing it — we were walking towards the one Lord, and thus towards one another [n. 28].

CHAPTER ELEVEN

Anti-Semitism and the Christian Bible: Interpretations and Misinterpretations

Originally given as an address on behalf of the Archdiocese of Denver and in cooperation with the American Jewish Committee of Colorado, on October 26, 2000.

Introduction

PERMIT ME TO GREET YOU with the words that Rabbi Yeshua used to announce His presence to His disciples on Easter night: *Shalom aleichem!* I do so fully agreeing with the powerful insight of Rabbi Joseph Soloveitchik: "A community is established the very moment I recognize the thou and extend greetings to the thou. One individual extends the 'shalom' greeting to another individual and in so doing he creates a community — recognition means sacrificial action: The individual who withdraws in order to make room for the thou."[65]

I also repeat those words of the Risen Christ, and in the original sacred language, not to impress or curry favor but because the words themselves and what they signify are at the very heart of my presentation this evening. And since an appreciation for storytelling is key to reading the Sacred Scriptures, I do not suppose that I require your indulgence to be a bit autobiographical at the outset. Indeed, I trust that I am merely being faithful to that Hebrew proverb that says, *"D'vorim hayotzim min ha-lev, nichnasim el ha-lev,"* which is stunningly close to the motto of the great Cardinal Newman, *"Cor ad cor loquitur"* ("Heart speaks to heart").

Although I grew up in what some might consider a "Catholic ghetto" in Newark, New Jersey, one cannot live in the Northeast without being in touch with Jews, in much the same way that Jews would be required to be in touch with Catholics in that same area. I guess my first contact with Jews came through my father, whose partners in his leather-finishing business were all Jews — albeit non-observant! We lived next to a Jewish physician and his wife; Mrs. Preston — also not observant — was a former schoolteacher, who took a shine to three-year-old Peter and was consistently interested in his educational progress until we moved away.

From my Lithuanian and Ukranian immigrant grandparents, I heard sad stories of the bosses and landlords they had when they first "got off the boat," people who made their life difficult and even sought to inhibit their practice of the Catholic Faith in ways, both subtle and direct; unfortunately, they were Jews. For thirteen years (from 1954 to 1968), I attended Catholic schools and in that entire time, I never heard a negative word about Judaism; whenever mentioned, something positive was said about Jews and their religion. Specifically, I should point out that no charge of deicide was ever uttered, nor was there any talk about a curse upon the Jewish people.

As a seventeen-year-old, I began my studies for the priesthood at Seton Hall University and had the incalculable joy of being introduced to Msgr. John Oesterreicher, the "granddaddy" of the Vatican II statement on the Jews; I served Mass for him several times a week, and we became lifelong friends. In 1971, I became the first graduate of the then-experimental program known as the Academy for Jewish Studies without Walls; the Jewish sponsors were delighted that their first protégé was a Catholic seminarian who had taken a course in the Old Testament from Samuel Sandmel of blessed memory.

From 1972 to 1975, I served at an inner-city parish elementary school in Trenton, New Jersey; across the street from us was a Hebrew Day School, with whom we had a wonderful relationship, including attending each other's services at least once a semester. After ordination, as a chaplain on a Caribbean cruise at Christmastime, I was asked by a group of Jewish tourists to lead their Hanukkah service — needless to say, they weren't Orthodox Jews!

From 1980 to 1985, I worked for the Catholic League for Religious and Civil Rights — the Catholic counterpart to the Anti-

Defamation League of B'nai B'rith. From an initial adversarial situation, we grew into a relationship of personal respect and, where possible, mutual support and cooperation. One of the great blessings of that time was developing a deep, personal friendship with Rabbi Leon Klenicki; I count him and his wife among my dearest friends to this day. He and I have collaborated on numerous projects, including co-authoring a book on Jewish-Catholic relations and several "dialogue" articles for the Catholic press.

Well, I think that should be enough to let you know about my long-standing interest, involvement, and commitment — lest you think Archbishop Chaput has brought in some kind of interreligious "carpetbagger"!

Our topic today is not for the fainthearted, and I do not intend to patronize you by serving up "tea and sympathy." I want to be honest and direct, even while being loving. Anything less accomplishes nothing, except either to antagonize or to raise false expectations. Our dialogue is too important to be so dishonored. I would like to divide my presentation into three main areas: (1) consideration of some fundamental propositions or presuppositions; (2) application of those foundational principles; and (3) reflection on problematic areas that remain. So, let's push forward together.

Propositions

On the first of June in 1980, during Pope John Paul II's first pastoral visit to France, he met with representatives of the Jewish community. He noted that "between Judaism and the Church, there is a relationship . . . 'at the very level of their respective religious identities.' " He continued: "This relationship must be further deepened and enriched by study, mutual knowledge, religious education on both sides, and the effort to overcome the difficulties that still exist." That's what we're about this evening, I trust.

The Pope also evoked the memory of a man whom he termed a "pioneer" in this endeavor, the Jewish-French historian Jules Isaac. Taking my cue from the Holy Father, I want to rely on the genius and inspiration of Jules Isaac, by using as "talking points" a series of "propositions" he highlighted in his 1949 work, *Jésus et Israël,* and subsequently translated into English in 1971 under the title of *Jesus and Israel.* I want to engage the revered scholar in a dialogue in which, for the most part, I will wholeheartedly endorse his conclusions but also disagree with respect where I feel compelled for either theological or historical reasons.

Nonetheless, I believe this list of twenty-one propositions is a good starting point for us all. As I share the thoughts of Dr. Isaac, I shall also comment on them (grouping some of his propositions together for ease in discussion); my hope is to provide Catholics present with a basic review of Catholic teaching in these areas and perhaps a bit of new information for Jews who are here.

PROPOSITION 1: The Christian religion is the daughter of the Jewish religion. The New Testament of the Christians is built upon the foundation of the Old Testament of the Jews. If only for this reason, Judaism is deserving of respect.

The first statement is no more than a historical truism to be accepted by anyone who values the truth. The second follows from it and has been consistently endorsed by the Catholic Church from time immemorial. When the second-century priest Marcion wanted to discard the Old Testament as worthless, the Church declared him a heretic. In the twentieth century, Pope Pius XI declared without fear of contradiction that Christians "are religious Semites." When we Catholics pray the First Eucharistic Prayer, or the Roman Canon, during the Sacred Liturgy, we bring to memory that the sacrifice we offer is done in continuity with all the sacrifices ever offered in salvation history, referring to Abraham as "our father in faith." Isaac thus argues that Judaism "is deserving of respect" for very practical reasons for Christian believers. Far more than that, however, Judaism "is deserving of respect" because it is a divinely revealed religion. As the Fathers of the Second Vatican Council reminded us:

> The Church cannot forget that she received the revelation of the Old Testament by way of that people with whom

God in his inexpressible mercy established the ancient covenant. Nor can she forget that she draws nourishment from that good olive tree onto which the wild olive branches of the Gentiles have been grafted.[66]

Cardinal Jean-Marie Lustiger, the Archbishop of Paris and Jewish convert to Catholicism, seconds the opinion of Dr. Isaac when he declares:

> For Christians, it is the Jews who are the living witnesses of the unique and historical character of Christian faith. It is impossible to understand anything about Christian belief if one does not accept God's choice of a Messiah, and one cannot understand God's choice of a Messiah if one does not accept His choice of Israel.[67]

PROPOSITION 2: Jesus, the Jesus of the Gospels, only Son and Incarnation of God for the Christians, in His human lifetime was a Jew, a humble Jewish artisan. This is a fact of which no Christian has a right to be unaware.

The point made is important and serious, but I can't resist sharing a somewhat humorous anecdote. I know a fellow who, from time to time, is less than enthusiastic about the Jewishness of Jesus. Whenever I say, "Remember, Tom, Jesus was a Jew," he replies, "Yes, Father, but only on His mother's side!" Of course, doctrinally speaking, he's correct, but somewhat ungraciously I press the point and recall that, according to Jewish law, it is precisely birth from a Jewish mother that makes one a Jew.

To return to the essential truth here, we need to underscore how the Christian belief in the doctrine of the Incarnation should influence everything. Indeed, we would say that from the beginning of time the Jewish race was blessed by God Who had the Incarnation in view and, needless to say, blessed ever since that central event.

This was clearly understood by someone like St. Bernard of Clairvaux in the twelfth century when some Crusaders thought a good "kickoff" to their trek east would be the destruction of all the

Jews they found en route. A thirteen-year-old Jewish boy gave his eyewitness account of Bernard's intervention:

> [He] calmed them, and said: "March towards Zion; defend the tomb of Christ. But touch not ye the Jews; speak to them with mildness: For they are the flesh and bones of the Messiah; and if you molest them, you will run the risk of touching the very apple of the Lord's eye!"[68]

PROPOSITION 3: Insofar as we can know of them through the Gospels, Jesus' family was Jewish: Mary, His mother, was Jewish, and so were all their friends and relatives. To be at once an anti–Semite and a Christian is to try to marry reverence with abuse.

This proposition is but a corollary of the first and rather self-evident. The non-Jews in the New Testament are rather few and far between, with the Roman centurion earning high marks and Pontius Pilate a failing grade. Jesus, in His earthly existence, grew — as the Gospels tell us — "and became strong, filled with wisdom; and the favor of God was upon him" (Lk 2:40). And He did so in a thoroughly Jewish environment that was filled with people of faith, from the shepherds of the Nativity (cf. Lk 2:8), to old Simeon and Anna (cf. Lk 2:25, 36), to his dear friends at Bethany (Martha, Mary, and Lazarus — cf. Jn 11:1), to the Twelve. We meet some Jews who were less than congenial, from Herod (whom Jesus calls "that fox" — cf. Lk 13:32) to Judas (His betrayer).

In the chiaroscuro of the Jewish religious landscape, fairness compels us to conclude that the lights far exceeded the shadows in their force and brilliance. All of this is simply to say that the faith of His holy mother and His foster father were not isolated examples of covenant fidelity, and that must be appreciated.

PROPOSITION 4: On each New Year's Day, the Church commemorates the circumcision of the Infant Jesus. It was not without hesitation and controversy that early Christianity abandoned this rite sanctioned by the Old Testament.

The feast referred to here has had many names, even in my own lifetime: The Lord's Circumcision; Octave Day of Christmas; and currently, Solemnity of Mary, Mother of God. The day recalls, however, the eighth day of Christ's earthly life when He was given His Name during the ancient ritual of circumcision.

Dr. Isaac refers with great respect to "the Infant Jesus" and with great accuracy to the crisis in the Early Church regarding circumcision. Nobody was actually opposed to the ceremony; the difficulty came because those who ended up being called "the Judaizers" had made a greater claim for the rite than it could bear. We find the record of it all in the fifteenth chapter of the Acts of the Apostles and in the second chapter of the Epistle to the Galatians. The supporters of maintaining circumcision and demanding it for Gentile converts to Christianity argued that salvation was not possible without it; Paul and others responded by noting that, if such were the case, the Cross of Christ would be eviscerated of its meaning. I do not believe any early Christian would have opposed circumcision if it had been treated within the community as an option, rather than as a necessity for salvation. To the present day, circumcision is practiced by many Christians, albeit generally for medical reasons.

To make a contemporary comparison for this debate, I would like to mention the schism of Archbishop Lefebvre and his followers, which most people assume has to do with the Latin Mass — which is certainly not the case. The late Archbishop was a great leader and thinker and made many valid points about the confusion that engulfed many portions of the Church after Vatican II. He got carried away by his own rhetoric, however, and made outrageous and unacceptable statements, culminating in his illicit consecration of four bishops and thus in his own automatic excommunication. With him, as with the Judaizers, the law of "progressive polemic" took over, giving what should have been a friendly, family debate a life of its own.

The bottom line, however, is rather simple: Christians have no objection to circumcision and are even free to see in it spiritual significance, for the sign of one covenant is not voided by another.

Therefore, as we offer the Lord's Body and Blood each day to His heavenly Father, we do it in continuity with the covenant first symbolized in salvation history by the rite of circumcision.

PROPOSITION 5: The name "Jesus Christ" is basically Semitic, even though its form is Greek: "Jesus" is a Hellenization of a Jewish name; "Christ" is the Greek equivalent of the Jewish word "Messiah."

In this item, we are given a little lesson in philology — and an important one. Most Christians fail to realize that "Jesus" — or really "Yeshua," or "Joshua" — was a very common Jewish name, meaning "God saves" or "God is the Savior," intended as an ongoing reminder of that foundational truth of Judaism. The title "Christ," on the other hand, translates the Hebrew *Mashiah*, signifying that the one so named was God's Anointed — the One to usher in the Kingdom. "Jesus the Christ," then, in His very Name recalls both His divine mission and His Jewish identity at one and the same time, for both come out of the Jewish experience of God's Revelation.

PROPOSITION 6: The New Testament was written in Greek. In the course of the centuries, the Catholic Church has quoted it in Latin, a Latin which is the result of translation. But Jesus, like all the Palestinian Jews He was addressing, spoke Aramaic, a Semitic language closely related to Hebrew.

While modern Christians may need to be reminded of this fact, it is highly significant that the first believers in Christ did not, for when the inspired authors sat down to write the New Testament, they felt almost compelled to maintain their "connectedness" to Judaism. They did this even to the point of keeping various words and expressions in the original Hebrew or Aramaic — the dialect commonly spoken in the Palestine of Christ's time.

And so, we find several examples of this in the Gospel of Mark (interestingly enough, written to Romans!): in 5:41, Jesus addresses the dead girl in Aramaic, *"Talitha cumi"* ("Little girl, I say to you, arise"); similarly, in 7:34, he cures the deaf man with the word

"Ephphatha!" ("Be opened"); of course, we can't forget Jesus' intimate address to the Father as *"Abba"* (really, closer to "Daddy" or
"Papa" than anything else), spoken during the Agony in the Garden
on the eve of His death (14:36); finally, the Evangelist at 15:34 pre-
serves Christ's last words on the Cross as the first line of Psalm 22,
"Eloi, Eloi, lama sabachthani?" ("My God, my God, why hast thou
forsaken me?").

The Church has held to that same instinct by using Hebrew
words in the Sacred Liturgy: *Alleluia* ("Praise the Lord"), *Hosanna*
("Grant your salvation"), and *Amen* ("So be it"). These are powerful
testimonies to the Jewish roots of Christianity and of our ongoing
acknowledgment of the same.

*PROPOSITION 7: It is commonly maintained that at the time of the
coming of Christ, the Jewish religion had degenerated into mere legalism
without a soul. History does not support this verdict. In spite of Jewish
legalism and its excesses, everything at this period attests to the depth and
intensity of the religious life of Israel.*

*PROPOSITION 9: Jesus was born and lived "under the [Jewish] law."
Did He intend or announce its abrogation? Many writers hold that He
did, but their statements exaggerate, distort, or contradict the most important passages in the Gospels.*

The seventh proposition takes head-on a common image of first-
century Judaism, one which is an unfortunate caricature. That there
was legalism in the Jewish religion at the time of Christ is certainly
true, but that everything about it was lifeless and desiccated is pa-
tently false. The soul of the Jewish religion was — and is — love, as
the *Shema* (confession of faith) makes a Jew remember every day. St.
Mark (12:29) depicts Christ Himself quoting Deuteronomy 6:4-5
to sum up the essence of true religion: "Hear, O Israel: The Lord our
God, the Lord is one; and you shall love the Lord your God with all
your heart, and with all your soul, and with all your mind, and with
all your strength." Jesus did not invent the law of love; He echoed it
and reminded everyone of it.

With regard to the Pharisees, we need to make several mental notes. First of all, from a doctrinal point of view, Jesus was a Pharisee; that is, He accepted and taught belief in the resurrection of the dead and in angels, and He advocated practices like fasting and almsgiving — hallmarks of Pharisaic doctrine and discipline. This may surprise many because the Gospels seem to indicate that Christ was involved in an apparently never-ending conflict with the Pharisees.

Which brings us to the second point: He was undoubtedly concerned about the legalism and even hypocrisy of some or many of the Pharisees, precisely because He believed they were "on track," doctrinally speaking. In other words, He bothered to correct them because He thought they were worth correcting. That's why, of course, we hear Him instructing His hearers to heed the teaching of "the scribes and Pharisees," even while He cautions against following their example — which could be off-base at various times (cf. Mt 23:2f). Indeed, He could not have been unimpressed by this lay reform movement begun for the very purpose of purifying Judaism and returning it to its pristine splendor.

Sometimes we listen to a line and don't really hear what's being said. One such verse of Matthew's Gospel contains Christ's warning: "Unless your righteousness [or "holiness," in some translations] exceeds that of the scribes and Pharisees, you will never enter the kingdom of heaven" (5:20). To be sure, this is not a rousing endorsement of Pharisaism, but it is not a rousing condemnation, either. Jesus says that one's holiness must "exceed" that "of the scribes and Pharisees," yes; but that means they did have some degree of holiness! That kernel of reality should always be kept in focus.

That leads us into our ninth proposition. That Jesus "was born and lived 'under the [Jewish] law' " is beyond dispute. Isaac is citing Galatians 4:4 to teach this fact. We know as well that Jesus was a pious Jew His whole life, frequenting both synagogue and Temple as required by traditional Jewish observance. Surely, He learned this attitude from His parents, who observed the Law with devotion, as we can glean from their bringing their infant Son to the Temple on the fortieth day after His birth (cf. Lk 2:22-24). St. Matthew is keen on informing us that Jesus "[had not] come to abolish the law and the prophets . . . but to fulfil them" (5:17). In the fifth chapter of St. Matthew's Gospel, Christ's six antitheses in the Sermon on the Mount ("You have heard that it was said . . . but I say to you . . .") were not contradictions of the Law but calls to do the maximum, rather than the minimum, to live a holy life. In truth, His very style was classically rabbinical as He "built a wall around the Torah" — a method of teaching that ensured that a truly serious offense would never be committed, by surrounding the value with earlier safeguards.

Catholics — and all other religious people — need to be reminded of the necessity of avoiding religious formalism, which can so easily devolve into a lifeless end in itself.

PROPOSITION 8: The teaching of Jesus took place in the traditional Jewish setting. According to a very liberal Jewish custom, "the carpenter's son" was permitted to speak and teach in the synagogues, and even in the Temple at Jerusalem.

PROPOSITION 10: Nothing would be more futile than to try to separate from Judaism the Gospel that Jesus preached in the synagogues and in the Temple. The truth is that the Gospel and its entire tradition are deeply rooted in Jewish tradition and in the attempts at renovation and purification that had been manifested for almost two centuries in Palestine.

These two statements are closely aligned with the two previous ones. As I just noted, Jesus was constantly found in traditional Jewish environments and sacred precincts; He was neither anti-cultic nor anti-institutional — a good corrective to serve up to such individuals today who try to use Him to justify their own agenda and behavior. As Dr. Isaac observes, Christ preached His message freely everywhere, including synagogues and the Temple, which means He was not teaching heresy from a Jewish perspective.

A historical note should be made here, too. When the definitive split occurred between rabbinic Judaism and the followers of "the Way" — that is, the Early Church — those disciples of Jesus took with them the standard synagogue service and merely added to it the re-presentation of Christ's Last Supper that took place, as we all know, in the context of the Passover. So, not only is any attempt to separate Judaism from the Gospel inadvisable, but it is downright destructive of the Gospel message and flies in the face of the practice of the Early Church. Furthermore, the fundamentals of Christianity — in its creed, code, and cult — are firmly rooted in Judaism.

PROPOSITION 11: Christian writers deliberately omit the fact that at the time of Christ the dispersion of the Jews had been a fait accompli for several centuries. The majority of the Jewish people no longer lived in Palestine.

PROPOSITION 12: Therefore, no one has any right to say that the Jewish people "as a whole" rejected Jesus. It is entirely probable that the Jewish people "as a whole" were not even aware of His existence.

PROPOSITION 13: But with rare exceptions, wherever Jesus went the Jewish people took Him to their hearts, as the Gospels testify. Did they, at a given moment, suddenly turn against Him? This is a notion that has yet to be proved.

PROPOSITION 14. In any case, no one has the right to declare that the Jewish people rejected Christ or the Messiah, that they rejected the Son of God, until it is proved that Jesus revealed Himself as such to the Jewish people "as a whole" and was rejected by them as such. But the Gospels give us good reason to doubt that this ever happened.

When Dr. Isaac asserts that "Christian writers deliberately omit," he is engaging in the very kind of generalization he finds offensive in many Christian sources. To say that "some" or "many" Christian writers do something is fine; to make a blanket statement is both untrue and unfair.

At any rate, the substance of his point is important — namely, that the dispersion of the Jews had preceded Christ's time by centuries and, therefore, can hardly be presented as a punishment for His rejection. Far more critical, however, is the warning not to hold that the Jewish people "as a whole" rejected Him; given the fact that the vast majority of the Jewish people lived outside Palestine, few would have even heard of Him, let alone come to a decision on Him one way or the other. And even within the Holy Land itself, we have no way of knowing percentages of folk who were touched by His message. We do know, however, that many who did hear and see Him were deeply moved, so much so that St. Luke tells us that the religious authorities hostile to Jesus were afraid to act against Him because of the support He had from the people (cf. 20:19).

Isaac raises the question as to how or why popular support for Jesus could turn into a mob reaction against Him — a logical question. Could that have happened? We know that crowds are fickle, but the scenario is highly unlikely. Did crowds clamor for His death? We Christians cannot doubt the truth of the Gospel words here, but that still does not translate into an act of the entire People of Israel; I don't think it far-fetched to suggest that those who would have appeared at such an event were opposed to Him already, while His supporters would not have graced such a travesty by their presence.

Regarding Christ's self-revelation, we do not know how much He said to whom and under what circumstances. Mark's Gospel abounds in instances of Christ's ordering His inner circle of disciples *not* to reveal His messianic identity to the masses, perhaps for fear of getting associated with the political aspects of the title in His time. Whatever the explanation, once more we cannot conclude that any revelation was made to Israel "as a whole," and hence, that there was a kind of communal rejection.

PROPOSITION 18: Joan of Arc was also sentenced by a tribunal of chief priests and scribes — who were not Jewish — but only after a long trial, of which we have the complete and authentic text. This is not true of the trial of Jesus, which was hurried through, whether in three hours or in three days, and is known only by hearsay. No official transcript, no contemporary testimony on the event has come down to us.

PROPOSITION 19: To establish the responsibility of the Jewish people in the Roman trial — the Roman death sentence — the Roman penalty, we must ascribe to certain passages in the Gospels a historical validity that is particularly dubious; we must overlook their discrepancies, their improbabilities, and give them an interpretation that is no less biased and arbitrary for being traditional.

On the first issue, we should say, "Good point." In truth, we know very little about the trial or trials of Jesus. If indeed the procedure alluded to in the Gospels was a full-blown trial at night, it was done in violation of Jewish law. I am afraid, however, that Isaac is a little looser in ascribing historical value to the Gospel accounts than I am — or the Catholic Church.

To speak of apparent "discrepancies" is fair enough, but that does not automatically render their "historical validity" "dubious." One thing of which we can be reasonably certain is that the Romans took no interest in the religious dimension of the battle between Jesus and Jewish religious authorities. That He claimed to be divine was of no interest to a people who already had a pantheon full of gods; their concern was related to any messianic assertions He might have made because those had serious political ramifications.

PROPOSITION 16: For eighteen hundred years, it has been generally taught throughout the Christian world that the Jewish people, in full responsibility for the Crucifixion, committed the inexpiable crime of deicide. No accusation could be more pernicious — and in fact none has caused more innocent blood to be shed.

PROPOSITION 20: To crown its injustices, a certain so-called Christian devotion, only too happy to fall in with a centuries-old prejudice which is complicated by ignorance or misunderstanding of the Gospel, has never wearied of using the grievous theme of the Crucifixion against the Jewish people as a whole.

In these two propositions, Dr. Isaac overstates the situation. To say that the charge of deicide was "generally taught" among Christians "for eighteen hundred years" is just not true. To speak of Christians "never [having] wearied" of such matters is a bit overdrawn. More crucial, however, is to realize that the teaching authority of the Church did not advance such a doctrine. For evidence of that, we need only look to the sixteenth-century Council of Trent, where, in speaking about Christ's saving Passion and Death, we read the following:

> We must regard as guilty all those who continue to relapse into their sins. Since our sins made the Lord Christ suffer the torment of the cross, those who plunge themselves into disorders and crimes crucify the Son of God anew in their hearts [for He is in them] and hold Him up to contempt. And it can be seen that our crime in this case is greater in us than in the Jews. As for them, according to the witness of the Apostle [Paul], "None of the rulers of this age understood this; for if they had, they would not have crucified the Lord of glory." We, however, profess to know Him. And when we deny Him by our deeds, we in some way seem to lay violent hands on Him.[69]

Admittedly, it cannot be doubted that individual Christians perpetuated the charge of deicide, not a few for political and/or economic advantage. But the whole Church cannot be held responsible for the actions of certain of her members, any more than all of Judaism can be held accountable for aberrations of certain of its adherents. When St. John Chrysostom — a great theologian and Father of the Church — spewed forth anti-Semitic venom, he was sinning and not offering the pure doctrine of the Catholic Church. When Sen. Joseph Lieberman adopts a so-called pro-choice position on abortion and is soft on the "gay" political agenda, he does not represent Orthodox Judaism, and everybody knows that — or should know it.

But allow me to make a contemporary application in the other direction: If Judaism "as a whole" does not wish to be condemned for the Death of Christ, in which only some of its members were complicit — and Judaism should not be condemned — nor should Christianity "as a whole" or the Church "as a whole" be held liable for the sinful actions or non-actions of certain would-be believers at the time of the Nazi Holocaust. The assignment of collective guilt is wrong whenever it is done and by everyone doing it. The Prophet Ezekiel teaches that clearly: "The son shall not suffer for the iniquity of the father, nor the father suffer for the iniquity of the son" (18:20).

So, whether we consider the Council of Trent or the Second Vatican Council, no one can claim Catholic support for a charge of deicide against the Jewish people. Therefore, in the final analysis, we must say simply: If any Catholic persists in accusing all Jews of the Death of Christ, that person is flying in the face of official Catholic teaching and cannot be considered a Catholic in good standing.

PROPOSITION 15: Christ is said to have pronounced a sentence of condemnation and alienation on the Jewish people. But why, in contradiction of His own Gospel of love and forgiveness, should He have condemned His own people, the only people to whom He chose to speak — His own people, among whom He found not only bitter enemies but fervent disciples and adoring followers? We have every reason to believe that the real object of His condemnation is the real subject of guilt, a certain pharisaism to be found in all times and in all peoples, in every religion and in every church.

PROPOSITION 17: Now, in the Gospels, Jesus was careful to name in advance the parties responsible for the Passion: elders, chief priests, scribes — a common species no more limited to the Jews than to any other people.

PROPOSITION 21 and Last: Whatever the sins of the People of Israel may be, they are innocent, totally innocent of the crimes of which Christian tradition accuses them: They did not reject Jesus; they did not crucify Him. And Jesus did not reject Israel, did not curse it: just as "the gifts . . . of God are irrevocable" (Rom 11:29), the evangelical Law of love allows no exception. May Christians come to realize this at last — may they realize and redress their crying injustices. At this moment, when a curse seems to weigh upon the whole human race, it is the urgent duty to which they are called by the memory of Auschwitz.

In Proposition 15, Jules Isaac brings us Christians up against the fundamental principle of the Gospel to love even our enemies. Without a doubt, the Jesus Who taught such unconditional love could not in the next breath condone or advocate hatred of an entire race. Furthermore, Isaac is on very firm ground when He reminds us that while Christ certainly had "bitter enemies" among the Jews, He also had "fervent disciples and adoring followers" among the same people — in fact, so much so that ten of the original Twelve ended giving up their lives to be faithful to Him and to His Gospel. St. Matthew is also careful to note that Jesus spoke of His primary concern being "the lost sheep of the house of Israel" (cf. 10:5f; 15:22-28). And when all is said and done, the most important statement emerges from the Gospel according to St. John, wherein we hear Jesus declare to the Samaritan woman that "salvation is from the Jews" (4:22)! This is an incredibly powerful assertion — and one which Christians can ignore only at great personal risk.

The seventeenth proposition calls for care in identifying the source of Jesus' problems, and here Isaac was merely a harbinger of the Vatican II document that spoke of the Jews, where we read: "Even though the Jewish authorities and those who followed their lead pressed for the death of Christ, neither all Jews indiscriminately at that time, nor Jews today, can be charged with the crimes committed during his passion." The bishops go on: "Consequently, all must take care, lest in catechizing or in preaching the Word of God, they teach anything which is not in accord with the truth of the Gospel message or the spirit of Christ."[70]

To be sure, we need to place the original conflict in perspective. Earlier on, I used the image of a family feud, which is what the debate between Temple Judaism and the followers of Christ really was. Pressure from within Judaism to maintain or reassert doctrinal purity and Roman oppression from without conspired to create an environment less tolerant of diversity than Judaism was historically known to countenance. With the murder of St. James and St. Stephen, a process had begun that culminated in the introduction of the nineteenth benediction (really a malediction) at the time of the rabbinic Council of Jamnia, making a formal schism almost inevitable. Once more, we find that the infamous law of progressive polemic had taken over, and unfortunately, when Christians were in a social and political position to retaliate, they did so, resulting in centuries of mutual animosity and finger-pointing, which is always counterproductive in human affairs.

In his final proposition, Isaac somewhat inaccurately speaks of "Christian tradition" accusing Jews. I hope it has become clear why I say he is being inaccurate. To evoke the memory of Auschwitz is incorrect, strained, and offensive. As many Jewish commentators have pointed out, when the Church was at the peak of her social and political power in the Middle Ages, European Jewry was not wiped out — even though it could have been accomplished with the flick of a papal pen. It was precisely during the nadir of Catholic power, under the thumb of an apostate Catholic who sought to destroy the Church and Judaism alike, that the People of the Covenant were marked out for the "final solution." Yosef Hayim Yerushalmi has observed that "there must be some significance in the fact that the Holocaust took place in our secular century, and *not* in the Middle Ages."[71]

Finally, Dr. Isaac brings forth Romans 11 as a witness in behalf of his position that God has not rejected the Jews, and he is absolutely correct — so correct that I would like to speak about St. Paul's understanding of the Jewish vocation in the world as a transition to the next phase of my reflections. At this moment, however, I think it only just to offer a hearty word of gratitude to Jules Isaac for offering us such worthwhile "food for thought." His understanding of Christianity and appreciation for it enabled him to find "common ground" on which to meet and, in this way, presents us all with the very example the Holy Father suggested as beneficial for our dialogue to advance.

Analysis of Some New Testament Texts

In discussions about alleged anti-Semitism in the New Testament, St. Paul's writings and the Gospel according to St. John are often brought forth as categorical evidence. I would like to argue the contrary. With that in mind, let us consider ever so briefly these two top contenders for the charge.

Chapters nine through eleven of St. Paul's Epistle to the Romans is, in my estimation, the essential key to unlock the mystery of salvation for Jews and Gentiles alike. Paul the Pharisaic rabbi reminds the Romans of some crucial facts of life, as he expresses his sorrow over the general Jewish rejection of Jesus as the Messiah, but doing so with great tenderness and even indicating his willingness to be lost himself than to have the then-current situation prevail, reminiscent of David's prayer that he could have died in place of his rebellious son Absalom (cf. 2 Sm 18:33):

1. Paul lists the glories of Judaism, and not in the past tense as some defective English translations present it. He argues, in typically rabbinic fashion, that the greatest glory is the physical descent of Jesus Christ from the stock of Israel (cf. 9:4f).

2. St. Paul goes on to argue that mere physical descent from Abraham does not constitute one a son of the covenant, but rather God's sovereign choice. To the charge that this appears unfair, the Apostle replies that this is human arrogance, writ large — a lesson obviously learned from old Job (cf. 9:6-24).

3. Paul continues his discourse by demonstrating that, in fact, this is not divine capriciousness, but part of the plan of God from all eternity, so that God's mercy might be revealed to the Gentiles. Thus, the apparent rejection of Christ by most of Judaism becomes a kind of holy excuse for God's offer of salvation to the *goyim*. St. Paul bolsters his point of view with a citation from the Prophet Joel: "*Every one* who calls upon the name of the Lord will be saved" (10:13; cf. Joel 2:32; emphasis added).

4. The presentation reaches crescendo in the eleventh chapter, as Paul asks pointedly if God has then rejected His people. He responds with a resounding, "By no means!" He asserts his own Jewishness in unequivocal terms and equates Jewish believers in Jesus with the "remnant" foretold by the prophets (11:1, 5).

5. Then Paul emphasizes the Gentile nature of his audience and declares that God has admitted them, "in order to make my fellow Jews jealous, and thus save some of them" (11:14). Next, he cautions the Gentiles in the Church at Rome against boasting about their status by forcefully reminding them that they are merely "a wild olive shoot" that has been grafted onto the "olive tree" (11:17), which is Israel. And, in case they miss it, he declares: "If you do boast, remember it is not you that support the root, but the root that supports you" (11:18).

6. Next, St. Paul issues a warning: "For if God did not spare the natural branches, neither will he spare you" (11:21). He also asserts that, in God's good time, the Jews will "be grafted back into their own olive tree" (11:24), which will happen — he says — when "the full number of Gentiles come in, and so all Israel will be saved" (11:25-26).

7. Paul teaches the Gentiles within that probably mixed Christian community of Rome that "as regards the gospel they [the Jews] are enemies of God, for your sake; but as regards election they are beloved for the sake of their forefathers [the patriarchs]." He concludes his analysis with a stunning flourish: "For the gifts and the call of God are irrevocable" (11:28-29).

8. Finally, reflecting on the entire mystery of election, Paul cries out:

> O the depth of the riches and wisdom and knowledge of God! How unsearchable are his judgments and how inscrutable his ways! "For who has known the mind of the Lord, or who has been his counselor?" "Or who has given a gift to him that he might be repaid?" For from him and through him and to him are all things. To him be glory forever. Amen [11:33-36].

The bottom line in all this is quite simple: St. Paul believes that at some future moment, the whole Jewish race will be given the grace to recognize Jesus as their long-awaited Lord and Messiah. Some Jews may bristle at the identification of Jesus of Nazareth with their longed-for Messiah, but not all. In a dialogue with Father Karl Rahner, the formidable Rabbi Pinchas Lapide said, "That he will be Jesus of Nazareth is a certainty for you and a not-to-be-precluded possibility for me."[72] But this is all intimately connected with God's covenant with Israel, so that He will not (and cannot) back out of it, precisely because His nature as God requires Him to be Fidelity personified. Last, but not least, the essence of the Pauline teaching is that salvation is a free gift of God to Jew and Gentile alike.

St. John's Gospel is often presented as an unrelenting screed against Judaism, but this cannot be maintained upon a more serious examination. The offending phrase generally cited is "the Jews," which more often than not has a negative connotation. I would like to submit that "the Jews" is, for the Evangelist, a kind of shorthand expression for those Jewish contemporaries of Christ who deliberately and willfully rejected Him with malice, and usually also to be equated with the religious leadership rather than the populace at large. On the other hand, when John wants to speak of the Chosen People of Jesus' day in a neutral or positive vein, he tends to speak of "Israel."

And so, we find John the Baptist proclaiming that he came to reveal the Messiah "to Israel" (1:31). Jesus pays an immense compliment to Nathanael by referring to him as "an Israelite indeed," and then adds, "in whom is no guile" (1:47). Nathanael returns the compliment by calling Jesus "the Son of God" and "the King of Israel" (1:49). And when Jesus wants to challenge Nicodemus to a more profound appreciation of the truth, he asks him — rhetorically — "You are a teacher of Israel, and yet you do not understand this?" (3:10). And, of course, we cannot ignore the critical passage noted earlier, that "salvation is from the Jews" (4:22).

Besides that, St. John is the sacred author who informs us of even leaders among the Jews who were disciples of Jesus, especially Nicodemus (3:1-15) and Joseph of Arimathea (19:38). St. John is also at pains to demonstrate Christ's intense desire to be viewed within the whole history of salvation in all its Jewishness (cf. 5:39; 5:46; 8:58; 12:41).

Far from being anti-Semitic, John's Gospel is arguably the most Jewish of the four. If there are hints of resentment found therein, I would hold that they result from hurt feelings from a very Jewish John, who finds it hard to comprehend why the heretofore pluralistic Judaism of the first century has become so closed in the case of Jesus. How could a Judaism that entertained the seemingly disparate positions of the Pharisees, Sadducees, Essenes, and Zealots not be equally open to the sect of Nazarenes, which (by the time of the composition of John's Gospel) had already been expelled from official Judaism? After all, to this day, Jews joke about placing ten Jews in a room and getting eleven opinions.

To be sure, the Roman occupation and the destruction of the Temple must be entered into the equation. This family feud, then, reflected in the pages of the Fourth Gospel, does not need to be purged but explained, which conviction caused A. T. Davies to call for honest study to "neutralize [the] potential for harm" from passages that could be construed as hostile to Judaism or Jews.[73]

Conclusion

As we come to the end of our investigation, I hope everyone (both Jew and Christian) can see clearly that anti-Semitism — like any other form of racism — is totally incompatible with the Gospel of Jesus Christ. That having been underscored, let us highlight a few specifics about Judaism and the New Testament:

1. First and most importantly, the New Testament contains works that, for us Christians, are sacred texts and part of Divine Revelation. If anti-Semitism is a form of racism and racism is a sin (which the Catholic Church teaches), then one cannot ascribe sinful attitudes to these sacred texts. That some texts have been taken as a pretext to validate prior prejudices is admissible; that they have been abused rather than used is also possible, but not the suggestion that anti-Semitism is endemic to the New Testament. Therefore, if anti-Semitism *seems* to be present, it must be only an appearance or misinterpretation and by no means inherent in the Sacred Text.

Hence, it is the responsibility of exegetes, preachers, and teachers to provide a proper explanation for passages that could be misinterpreted or even have been treated so in the course of the centuries. In other words, it is not our prerogative to strike from Sacred Scripture what we find problematic, but rather to understand it correctly and then to share that understanding with others — a point made by no less a scholar and committed ecumenist than the late Father Raymond E. Brown, in his work *The Community of the Beloved Disciple*. This was likewise the approach of Samuel Sandmel, in his volume *Anti-Semitism in the New Testament?* His conclusion is that while one can find a polemic and an apologetic against Judaism in certain New Testament pericopes, this does not constitute an abiding or necessary element of the Christian Tradition.

2. Christian instruction should not whitewash difficulties that either Jesus or the Early Church had with the religious establishment of first-century Judaism, but it is equally important to offer examples of the positive interaction recorded in the New Testament: for example, by demonstrating how Jesus' positions on divorce and remarriage and other matters were rather faithful reflections of the branch of Pharisees led by Hillel; by noting that St. Luke is careful to record that on certain occasions Pharisees attempted to save the lives of both Jesus (cf. Lk 13:31) and the apostles (cf. Acts 5:34-39) — with Gamaliel, in the latter example, reminding the Sanhedrin of the need for patience and justice in regard to the fledgling Christian movement, still within Judaism; or by showing that Joseph of Arimathea and Nicodemus — both religious leaders within Judaism — are loyal to Jesus, even to the point of requesting His body from Pilate under very precarious circumstances (cf. Jn 19:38-39).

3. Catholics consider that they have a unique bond with Jews, signified by the fact that the official dialogue agency between the Holy See and Judaism is not, as one might suppose, the Pontifical Council for Interreligious Dialogue (to deal with non-Christian

religions like Islam, Buddhism, and Hinduism), but the Pontifical Council for Promoting Christian Unity. However, from the other side, it is important to observe that Catholics actually have more in common with Judaism than other Christian bodies do, most particularly in our refusal to rely on Scripture alone. Indeed, as Hyam Maccoby notes:

> For the Talmud was the direct analogue of the main institutions by which the Church claimed to be the guardian and interpreter of the scriptural revelation. The legal parts of the Talmud correspond to the Christian canon law. The stories of the rabbis correspond to the Christian hagiographies, and the Talmudic biblical homilies and exegesis correspond to the similar works of exegesis, exhortation and reflection in the Early Fathers and scholastics.[74]

This highlights the responsibility of the Catholic Church to use well and wisely her magisterial authority to offer interpretations of Sacred Scripture in keeping with the highest standards of exegesis and grounded in the foundational principles of the Gospel message. For better or worse, Judaism no longer has a magisterial mechanism, but I would urge the establishment of venues and forums that approximate it, especially as regards the informing of Jewish attitudes toward Christianity. Public opinion polls tell us that prior to Pope John Paul's visit to Israel, the average Jew had only the foggiest understanding of Christianity, and that was based mostly on outmoded stereotypes from the Middle Ages! Surely, this is what the 170 Jewish scholars intended to target in their *New York Times* ad of September 10, 2000, when they declared: "We believe it is time for Jews to learn about the efforts of Christians to honor Judaism. We believe it is time for Jews to reflect on what Judaism may now say about Christianity."

4. Not infrequently, Jews express displeasure or even offense at Christian references to the *Tanakh* as "the Old Testament," which

they regard as a particularly egregious example of what is often termed "fulfillment language." Let's look at each in turn.

Why do we insist on speaking of the "Old Testament," especially when we know it causes discomfort? Alternatives have been suggested like "Hebrew Bible" or "Hebrew Scriptures," but these cannot suffice for various reasons. First of all, what Catholics and Orthodox Christians intend by "Old Testament" does not correspond exactly to what Jews today consider their Bible. The Pontifical Biblical Commission explains it clearly and simply: "The Christian Church has received as 'Old Testament' the writings which had authority in the Hellenistic Jewish community, but some of these are either lacking in the Hebrew Bible or appear there in somewhat different form."[75] In other words, the early Christian community adopted as Scripture not the Bible in use in first-century Palestine but the Greek version employed by Diaspora Judaism, the canon of which is seven books longer, with some of those texts not even having a parallel in Hebrew.

But more to the point, as the Vatican Commission for Religious Relations with the Jews explained fifteen years ago, "We continue to use the expression 'Old Testament' because it is traditional (cf. 2 Cor 3:14) but also because 'Old' does not mean 'out of date' or 'outworn.' In any case, it is the *permanent* value of the Old Testament as a source of Christian Revelation that is emphasized here (cf. *Dei Verbum*, 3) [emphasis in original]."[76] That having been said, the Pontifical Biblical Commission actually encourages "recourse to Jewish traditions of interpretation" and cautions against any kind of use of the Old Testament that would see significance in it only in relation to the New. We read: "One must respect each stage of the history of salvation. To empty out of the Old Testament its own proper meaning would be to deprive the New of its roots in history."[77]

Now, on to the somewhat sensitive topic of "fulfillment" notions and, specifically, the so-called typological method of exegesis. Typology is a classical method of Christian exegesis, inherited from Judaism, seeing in earlier events or persons a forerunner of yet greater realities to come. Thus, traditional Christian interpretation views the manna of the wilderness and the Passover supper as brought to an even higher level by the Christian Eucharist, wherein we believe Jesus Christ feeds us with His own Body and Blood. That does not mean that the manna or the Passover in their original appearances are thus emptied of value; on the contrary, their meaning is completely maintained and, as a matter of fact, what we consider to be so important would have no value if their "types" or "foreshadowings" had none, either to begin with or at present.

Similarly, certain New Testament authors and Fathers of the Church speak of the Church as the "New Israel." That should not be understood as negating the earlier relationship between God and His People before Christ's coming, nor should it be regarded as doing so in the present — as we have already seen in our study of Romans 9-11.

However, lest Jews imagine that Christians are irremediably arrogant, it is good to realize that we do not believe that our own sacred realities will have a permanent existence as we presently experience them, either. Thus, as sacred as the Eucharist is to us Catholics, we believe that it is but a foreshadowing of what is yet to come, to be fulfilled in the Paschal Feast of Heaven.

In the same way, although we firmly hold that Jesus Christ established the Church as the extension of His Incarnation through space and time, we also believe that the seeds of the Kingdom that flower in the Church here below will be brought to a glorious blossoming only in the eschatological Kingdom. So, my Jewish friends, do not think we Christians ascribe a time-bound significance for you while holding to a timeless one for ourselves. No, we would say that all of us have to be fulfilled and ought to be looking forward to it.

5. Finally, I would plead for a cessation of a conversation (which really devolves into a monologue) rooted in mutual recriminations, reminiscent of children on a playground arguing over who started the fight. That anti-Semitic commentaries have colored Christian approaches to Jews is undeniable. Equally undeniable, however, is that Jewish texts, including the Talmud, are not exactly top con-

tenders for retiring wallflowers in the art exercised in the reverse, with some vicious and vitriolic statements made about Jesus as a sorcerer and idolater (cf. b Sanh., 43a) now "suffering in hell by being immersed in boiling excrement" (b Gitt, 56b) or about the alleged promiscuity of the Virgin Mary (cf. b Sanh., 67a). Maccoby candidly admits, with admirable understatement, "These passages [in the Talmud] are certainly not complimentary."[78] I mention these instances only to show how futile "digging for dirt" can be.

We Catholics have been immersed in a Jubilee Year, hearing in countless ways the ancient biblical call for *teshuvah*. In the Holy Year of 1950, Pope Pius XII invited the Jews of his time to join the Catholic Church for the celebration. Although the language he used would not be deemed totally "apt" today, it did signal the beginning of a new moment. He said: "We open the holy door to all who worship Christ, not excluding those who await His coming in good faith though in vain, and honor Him as the One Whom the Prophets proclaimed who has yet to come. We offer them a fatherly greeting and welcome."[79]

In that same mentality, I would like to renew the invitation: Let us confess our sins against each other. Let us seek the forgiveness of each other. Let us begin again. I hope we will embark on this path of *teshuvah* together and in the spirit of "sacrificial action" called for by Rabbi Soloveitchik, whom I cited in my opening remarks.

Whether by a happy coincidence or by Divine Providence, Jews around the world have just celebrated Simchat Torah, the feast of rejoicing in the Torah, during which one takes the Torah under one's arm like a bride and dances with it around the synagogue. This is the response we all — Catholics and Jews both — should have to the presence and the challenge of God's holy Word, what we both consider to be the Sacred Scriptures. The result will be the joyful proclamation: *Adonai, Elohei, Yisrael, Melekh; u–malkhuto bakol mashalah* ("The Lord, the God of Israel is King; His reign embraces all that is").

Baruch haShem Adonai! ("Blessed be the Name of the Lord!")

CHAPTER TWELVE

~~~

Dominus Iesus and the
Third Millennium

"ALL RELIGIONS TEACH people to be good."

"Jesus was a great teacher, just like Buddha and the founders of other religions."

"As a missionary, I don't go to a foreign country to make people Catholics; I hope my presence makes them better Buddhists or Hindus."

Statements like the above were responsible for the issuance of a document by the Congregation for the Doctrine of the Faith on August 6, 2000 — *Dominus Iesus* ("The Lord Jesus"). Aside from *Humanae Vitae* in 1968, I cannot recall any other ecclesiastical text to raise such a brouhaha. And like the 1968 encyclical, I found people reacting to the one in 2000 without ever having read the work itself. The most negative comments came from non-Catholic Christian leaders who wondered aloud whether ecumenism was now a dead issue as far as the Catholic Church is concerned. So just what did *Dominus Iesus* say?

Four months to the day of its promulgation, I was attending a meeting of a diocesan ecumenical commission, whose entire agenda on that occasion had been dedicated to a discussion of *Dominus Iesus*, in an effort to calm ecumenical fears and to assuage feelings of hurt and anger. One after another, non-Catholic representatives expressed their anger, disappointment, or shock — until we got to an Assemblies of God minister. Allow me to paraphrase his summation: "As I read the document, it says two things. First, that Jesus Christ is the way to salvation for the entire human race. I believe that completely, and I thought every other Christian did, too. Second, that the Catholic Church believes that it is the unique means of putting the human race into contact with Christ and His saving

Gospel. I do not believe that, which is why I am not a Catholic. And if a Catholic does not believe that, I don't know why he's still a Catholic. I happen to believe that about the Assemblies of God, which is why I am a member." He got it right, in my estimation.

Now, let's take a brief look at the declaration of the Congregation for the Doctrine of the Faith.

First of all, for whom was/is it intended? It is an intensely theological document, and internal to the Catholic Church. In other words, it was not aimed at "the person in the pew," much less at an ecumenical audience. Therefore, the tone does not come across as pastoral or conciliatory; it has the resonances of science.

Second, what's new in it? Absolutely nothing. Furthermore, the points made are all grounded not only in the Tradition but also in the conciliar and post-conciliar Magisterium. Amazingly, by my count, only 14 of the 102 footnotes come from texts before Vatican II — and even several of them are used to substantiate post-conciliar approaches.

What is contained in the document? It is relatively brief (just thirty pages in the edition I have), with six chapters, dealing with: (1) the fullness and definitiveness of the Revelation of Jesus Christ; (2) the incarnate *Logos* and the Holy Spirit in the work of salvation; (3) unicity and universality of the salvific mystery of Jesus Christ; (4) unicity and unity of the Church; (5) the Church: Kingdom of God and Kingdom of Christ; (6) the Church and the other religions in relation to salvation.

What are the fundamental truths taught here?

- In Christ, the Father has spoken His final and definitive Word of Revelation.
- Jesus Christ as true God and true Man is the *Logos*, in Whose Incarnation and Paschal Mystery is accomplished the redemption of the entire human race.
- The Church was established by Jesus Christ as *the* means of salvation, containing within itself the seeds of the Kingdom, which shall come to its consummation at the eschaton.

- Just as "there is salvation in no other name" than Jesus', so salvation is mediated in a unique manner by the Catholic Church.

What did the declaration *not* say?

- That other religions are false or evil.
- That other Christian bodies cannot assist in the salvation of their members.
- That non-Catholics, whether Christian or not, cannot be saved.

What are the most neuralgic issues? It seems that some respondents balked at the notion that *Dominus Iesus* was apparently saying that the Catholic Church is the one true Church. But that was explicitly taught at Vatican II, in documents like the Declaration on Religious Liberty (n. 1), the Dogmatic Constitution on the Church (n. 8), and — of all places — the Decree on Ecumenism (n. 3)! If the idea of the uniqueness of the Church has been so consistently taught, up to and including Vatican II, what's the problem? Probably that this teaching has been lost in the shuffle of ecumenical or interfaith euphoria, and the Congregation saw a need to remind Catholics that this is still part and parcel of our Faith.

A second "offensive" remark in the declaration is that ecclesial communities that lack a valid episcopate "are not Churches in the proper sense" (n. 17). Again, this is merely a restatement of the teaching of the Second Vatican Council. Indeed, the very reason the Council Fathers came up with the expression "ecclesial communities" was to distinguish those bodies that had maintained the historic episcopate from those that had not; the new expression was an attempt at according some kind of "ecclesiality" to those lacking valid Orders, all the while holding to the constant teaching that to be a Church "in the proper sense" demands valid Orders and thus a valid Eucharist.

Which brings us to a third item: the "defects" of various ecclesial communities. Part of the difficulty is semantic. When we hear "defect" or "defective" in English, we tend to think of deformities or ineffectuality. Theologically, it simply means a lack. When *Dominus Iesus* says that these bodies "suffer from defects," it is actually quoting Vatican II's Decree on Ecumenism. And all it means is that they lack the *fullness* of the means of salvation, not that they cannot serve as vehicles of grace. No Baptist or Presbyterian, for instance, should be offended or surprised to discover that the Catholic Church believes maintenance of the Sacrament of Orders belongs to the very essence of the life of the Church, and that these bodies — by their own free choice and theological conviction — do not believe that. Of course, that's why they are Protestants to begin with.

Finally, what about other religions? Does *Dominus Iesus* give "short shrift" to them? Once more, the declaration simply sums up the constant teaching of the Church: Jesus Christ is the Way, the Truth, and the Life; therefore, He and the Church He founded are the ordinary, normal means of salvation; the Catholic Church rejoices in the truth taught in any religion but must also judge such teachings in the light of the definitive Revelation of Jesus Christ; men may be saved in any religion, if they are sincerely following the voice of conscience; when such people are saved, they are saved — whether they know it or not — by Jesus Christ and His Church. However, since no one can know for certain that he is saved, except in a direct and conscious relationship with Christ and His Church, the Gospel must be proclaimed to every creature, with the explicit goal of conversion.

Why was the declaration written? First, "as a remedy for [a] relativistic mentality, which is becoming ever more common" (n. 5). But second, also to aid genuine dialogue: "to set forth again the doctrine of the Catholic faith in these areas, pointing out some fundamental questions that remain open to further development, and refuting specific positions that are erroneous or ambiguous. For this reason, the Declaration takes up what has been taught in previous Magisterial documents, in order to reiterate certain truths that are part of the Church's faith" (n. 3).

Less than a month after the release of the declaration, Pope John Paul II felt compelled to "weigh in" on it. Since some commentators had alleged that Cardinal Ratzinger had exceeded his authority in producing the text or had even acted at variance with the Pope's own desires, the Holy Father put that rumor to rest and then offered his personal rationale for it: "With the Declaration *Dominus Iesus* — Jesus is Lord — approved by me in a special way at the height of the Jubilee Year, I wanted to invite all Christians to renew their fidelity to him in the joy of faith and to bear unanimous witness that the Son, both today and tomorrow, is 'the way, the truth, and the life' (Jn 14:6)." This Christian profession, the Pope argues, "is not arrogance that disdains other religions, but joyful gratitude that Christ has revealed himself to us without any merit on our part." He continues: "At the same time, he has obliged us to continue giving what we have received and to communicate to others what we have been given, since the Truth that has been given and the Love that is God belong to all people." As the Pope sees it, then, sharing the Gospel with others is an act of gratitude to Almighty God and equally an act of charity toward our fellow man.

John Paul II concludes by expressing the hope "that this Declaration, which is close to my heart, can, after so many erroneous interpretations, finally fulfill its function both of clarification and of openness." The irony, of course, is that the declaration's original intent was to confront "erroneous" opinions but ended up itself being the victim of "erroneous interpretations." The document ends by noting that "theological reflection is called [for] to reconfirm the Church's faith and to give reasons for her hope in a way that is convincing and effective" (n. 23).

With impressive consistency, then, we find the Church down the centuries affirming the same two basic doctrines we considered in the first chapter of this book: the uniqueness of Jesus Christ and the necessity of the Church. What we have received, we must hand on (cf. 1 Cor 15:3). A failure to do so is to neglect one's baptismal vocation and to deny to others the certitude of their eternal salvation. Personal conviction about the truth of Christianity leads one — inexorably and humbly — to engage in the work of evangelization, which Pope John Paul II has tirelessly proclaimed to be the primary mission of the Church of the Third Millennium:

> The missionary mandate accompanies us into the Third Millennium and urges us to share the enthusiasm of the very first Christians: we can count on the power of the same Spirit who was poured out at Pentecost and who impels us still today to start out anew, sustained by the hope "which does not disappoint" (Rom 5:5) [*Novo Millennio Ineunte,* n. 58].

ENDNOTES

1. When I asked my mother what an Anglican was, she replied, "Oh, they just go to Mass in English!" Admittedly, the differences between Anglicanism and Catholicism were far greater than the language of the Sacred Liturgy, but regrettably, those differences are far more profound today than forty years ago.

2. Francis A. Sullivan, *Salvation Outside the Church? Tracing the History of the Catholic Response* (Mahwah, N.J.: Paulist Press, 1992).

3. Denzinger-Schönmetzer (hereafter DS), 792.

4. Ibid., 802.

5. Ibid., 870.

6. Ibid., 875.

7. Ibid., cf. 1351, 1870, 2865, 2867.

8. *Lumen Gentium*, n. 14.

9. *First Apology*, 46.

10. *Letter to Philadelphians*, 3:3.

11. *Epist.*, 4:4.

12. *Epist.*, 73:21.

13. *In Psalm.*, 118, *Sermo* 8:57.

14. *Oratio Catechetica*, 30.

15. *In Epist. ad Rom. Hom.*, 26:3-4.

16. *De Vocatione*, 2:17.

17. *Summa Theologiae* (hereafter *ST*), III, q. 68, a. 2.

18. *ST*, I-II, q. 89, a. 6.

19. DS, 875.

20. Pars 2, cap. 32.

21. DS, 1351.

22. *"De Indis et de Jure Belli Relationes"* in *Classics of International Law*, 142.

23. *De Libero Hominis Arbitrio*, lib. X, fol. 181 r-v.

24. Ibid.

25. DS, 1925.

26. Ibid., 1068.

27. Ibid., 2305.

28. Ibid., 2308.

29. Ibid., 2311.

30. Ibid., 3872.

31. Sullivan, p. 161.

32. General audience (Nov. 15, 1989).

33. *De Baptismo*, V, 27.38. A similar point is made in his *De Civitate Dei*, I, 35, and in an earlier place in *De Baptismo*, IV, 10.17. Furthermore, in his discourse on Psalm 32, Augustine points out the intricacies involved here: "We entreat you, brothers, as earnestly as we are able, to have charity, not only for one another, but also for those who are outside the Church. Of these, some are still pagans, who have not yet made an act of faith in Christ. Others are separated insofar as they are joined with us in professing faith in Christ, our Head, but are yet divided from the unity of His Body. My friends, we must grieve over these as over our brothers. Whether they like it or not, they are our brothers; and they will only cease to be so when they no longer say 'our Father.'"

34. Suzanne Martineau in *Pédagogie de l'Œcuménisme* (Paris: Fayard-Mame, 1965), p. 268.

35. Lewis T. Wattson became Father Paul of Graymoor, reestablishing Anglican religious life and leading his entire community of men and women into full communion with Rome — the first such occurrence since the Reformation.

36. Quoted by Pastor Hébert Roux in *De la Désunion vers la Communion*, 1981.

37. In this regard, it is worth consulting the first chapter of this book, "The Necessity of the Church," dealing with the doctrine of "*extra Ecclesiam*," to see how *Lumen Gentium* developed the teaching on full and imperfect communion.

38. The reader will notice a heavy emphasis on ecumenical accomplishments in the early period, and with good reason, for the efforts and results then laid the foundation for subsequent endeavors, which have been numerous and are easily accessible in a variety of other sources.

39. "Ecumenism," *Sacramentum Mundi* (New York: Crossroad, 1968), p. 199.

40. See, for instance, his strong statement in *Ut Unum Sint*, n. 3.

41. "Another Step Forward on the Road to Ecumenism," *L'Osservatore Romano* (Nov. 4, 1971), p. 2.

42. For a complete treatment of the above events, cf. *Report on the Ecumenical Situation 1970*, published by the Secretariat for Promoting Christian Unity, pp. 3-8.

43. Secretariat for Promoting Christian Unity, Op. cit., p. 8.

44. Ibid., p. 7.

45. "Reflections and Suggestions Concerning Ecumenical Dialogue," *Crux Special* (Oct. 9, 1970), p. 3.

46. For the complete text of these statements, cf. *Catholic Mind* (April 1971), pp. 35-50.

47. In a worldwide context, the Lutheran-Catholic dialogue brought about the Agreed Statement on Justification, on Oct. 31, 1999. Although not resolving all the thorny questions on this "hot-button" topic of the Reformation, the document did go a long way toward providing a great deal of common ground on which to base future conversations.

48. *Evangelicals and Catholics Together: The Christian Mission in the Third Millennium* is a statement that was released in May 1994, of unofficial status but a witness to the vision held in common, particularly in regard to the task of Gospel-rooted Christians in terms of society-at-large.

49. James Walsh, S.J. (ed.), *The Mind of Paul VI* (Milwaukee: Bruce Publishing Co., 1964), p. 265.

50. H.E. Cardinale, *Signs of the Times and Ecumenical Aspirations* (London, 1967), p. 26.

51. *Report on the Ecumenical Situation 1970,* p. 39.

52. Thomas C. Oden, *Requiem: A Lament in Three Movements* (Nashville, Tenn.: Abingdon Press, 1995), p. 82.

53. So wrote St. Ignatius of Antioch around A.D. 110, in his *Epistle to the Romans.*

54. Thomas Stransky, C.S.P., *The Decree on Ecumenism* (Glen Rock, N.J.: Paulist Press, 1965), p. 14.

55. The history of celibacy is often a contentious point between East and West. What is certainly clear is that while the East did indeed continue to ordain married men to the priesthood, it required of them and their wives a life of continence after ordination. For a good summary of this situation, see Peter M.J. Stravinskas, Ph.D., S.T.D. (ed.), *Priestly Celibacy: Its Scriptural, Historical, Spiritual, and Psychological Roots* (Mount Pocono, Pa.: Newman House Press, 2001). More detailed historical studies can be found in Christian Cochini, S.J., *The Apostolic Origins of Priestly Celibacy* (San Francisco: Ignatius Press, 1990).

56. Philip Caraman, S.J. (ed.), "The Church as a Visible Institution," *The Pastoral Sermons of Ronald A. Knox* (New York: Sheed & Ward, 1960), p. 99.

57. One should not fail to see how the Pope is careful to speak of the sins against unity of the *members* of the Church, rather than of the Church

herself. This is a critical distinction since the Church is, as St. Paul teaches, the sinless bride of Christ, albeit composed of sinful members.

58. Here the Pope is referring to the fact that he publicly professed the Creed without the "Filioque" clause, which has been a neuralgic issue for the Orthodox for centuries. In the Catholic view of things — and then as a result of Orthodox-Catholic dialogue, for the Orthodox as well — it is recognized that the Creed with or without that clause can be understood in a doctrinally correct manner. This was the Pope's symbolic gesture toward the East in this regard.

59. Here the Pope offers as examples ecumenical translations of the Bible; liturgical renewal, especially evident as various Reformation communities have rediscovered the centrality of the Eucharist; and adoption of a common lectionary. He ends this section by asking, "A century ago who could even have imagined such a thing?" (n. 45). This is critical to underscore for some Catholics who petulantly argue that "we" Catholics have made all the changes, with no corresponding moves from the other side.

60. Under this heading, the Holy Father makes special mention of the Christian martyrs of the twentieth century from the entire spectrum of Churches and communities. In the United States, how could we fail to note how the pro-life cause has broken down barriers, especially between Catholics and Evangelicals, as both have given a unified witness to the sanctity of human life, marching shoulder-to-shoulder and even sharing jail cells?

61. In this category, the Pontiff lists the numerous encounters his immediate predecessors and he have had with the various hierarchs of the Eastern Churches, all seen as instances of his desire that the Church "breathe with both lungs" (n. 54). He also cites documents from his own pontificate: *Slavorum Apostoli*, on Sts. Cyril and Methodius (1985), and *Euntes in Mundum* (1988), to commemorate the millennium of the Baptism of Kievan Rus.

62. It should be noted that the expression "sister Churches" can only be used of those bodies that have retained apostolic succession, thus possessing valid Orders and, therefore, a valid Eucharist.

63. This became all the more so with the effective demise of priestly celibacy among the secular clergy in the East. As a result, monasticism became the preserver and standard-bearer of liturgy, theology, spirituality, and even culture.

64. The apophatic way is a method of theological discourse holding that it is easier to say what God is not, rather than what He is. The Lit-

urgy of St. John Chrysostom, for example, speaks of God as "ineffable, inconceivable, invisible, incomprehensible." St. Thomas Aquinas, in the West, was also enamored of this approach.

65. Joseph Soloveitchik, "The Community," *Tradition* (Spring 1978).

66. *Nostra Aetate*, n. 4.

67. Jean-Marie Cardinal Lustiger, *Dare to Believe* (New York: Crossroad Publishing Co., 1986), p. 50.

68. Text from the anonymous translation of the classic biography by Ratisbonne, *The Life and Times of St. Bernard* (New York, 1902), p. 361.

69. *Roman Catechism*, I, 5, 11.

70. *Nostra Aetate*, n. 4.

71. Yosef Hayim Yerushalmi, *Auschwitz: Beginning of a New Era?* (New York: KTAV/ADL, 1977), p. 103.

72. Cited in Leon Klenicki and Richard John Neuhaus, *Believing Today: Jew and Christian in Conversation* (Grand Rapids, Mich.: Eerdmans Publishing Co., 1989), p. 87.

73. A.T. Davies, *Anti-Semitism and the Foundations of Christianity* (New York: Paulist Press, 1979), p. xv.

74. Hyam Maccoby et al. (eds.), *Judaism on Trial* (London: The Littman Library of Jewish Civilization, 1993), p. 20.

75. Pontifical Biblical Commission, *The Interpretation of the Bible in the Church* (Vatican City State: Libreria Editrice Vaticana, 1993), p. 52.

76. Commission for Religious Relations with the Jews, *Notes on the Correct Way to Present Jews and Judaism in Preaching and Catechesis in the Roman Catholic Church* (June 24, 1985), footnote 1.

77. Pontifical Biblical Commission, p. 53.

78. Maccoby, p. 26.

79. Cited in John M. Oesterreicher, *The New Encounter between Christians and Jews* (New York: Philosophical Library, 1986), p. 117.

APPENDIX

―≈―

Dominus Iesus

(Declaration on the Unicity and Salvific Universality of Jesus Christ and the Church)

Congregation for the Doctrine of the Faith

Introduction

1. The *Lord Jesus*, before ascending into heaven, commanded his disciples to proclaim the Gospel to the whole world and to baptize all nations: "Go into the whole world and proclaim the Gospel to every creature. He who believes and is baptized will be saved; he who does not believe will be condemned" (Mk 16:15-16); "All power in heaven and on earth has been given to me. Go therefore and teach all nations, baptizing them in the name of the Father, and of the Son, and of the Holy Spirit, teaching them to observe all that I have commanded you. And behold, I am with you always, until the end of the world" (Mt 28:18-20; cf. Lk 24:46-48; Jn 17:18, 20, 21; Acts 1:8).

The Church's universal mission is born from the command of Jesus Christ and is fulfilled in the course of the centuries in the proclamation of the mystery of God, Father, Son, and Holy Spirit, and the mystery of the incarnation of the Son, as saving event for all humanity. The fundamental contents of the profession of the Christian faith are expressed thus: "I believe in one God, the Father, Almighty, maker of heaven and earth, of all that is, seen and unseen. I believe in one Lord, Jesus Christ, the only Son of God, eternally begotten of the Father, God from God, Light from Light, true God from true God, begotten, not made, of one being with the Father. Through him all things were made. For us men and for our salvation, he came down from heaven: by the power of the Holy Spirit he became incarnate of the Virgin Mary, and became man. For our sake he was crucified under Pontius Pilate; he suffered death and was buried. On the third day he rose again in accordance with the Scriptures; he ascended into heaven and is seated at the right hand of the Father. He will come again in glory to judge the living and the dead, and his kingdom will have no end. I believe in the Holy Spirit, the Lord, the giver of life, who proceeds from the Father. With the Father and the Son he is worshipped and glorified. He has spoken through the prophets. I believe in one holy catholic and apostolic Church. I acknowledge one baptism for the forgiveness of sins. I look for the resurrection of the dead, and the life of the world to come."[1]

2. In the course of the centuries, the Church has proclaimed and witnessed with fidelity to the Gospel of Jesus. At the close of the second millennium, however, this mission is still far from complete.[2] For that reason, Saint Paul's words are now more relevant than ever: "Preaching the Gospel is not a reason for me to boast; it is a necessity laid on me: woe to me if I do not preach the Gospel!" (1 Cor 9:16). This explains the Magisterium's particular attention to giving reasons for and supporting the evangelizing mission of the Church, above all in connection with the religious traditions of the world.[3]

In considering the values which these religions witness to and offer humanity, with an open and positive approach, the Second Vatican Council's Declaration on the relation of the Church to non-Christian religions states: "The Catholic Church rejects nothing of what is true and holy in these religions. She has a high regard for the manner of life and conduct, the precepts and teachings, which, although differing in many ways from her own teaching, nonetheless often reflect a ray of that truth which enlightens all men."[4] Continuing in this line of thought, the Church's proclamation of Jesus Christ, "the way, the truth, and the life" (Jn 14:6), today also makes use of the practice of interreligious dialogue. Such dialogue certainly does not replace, but rather accompanies the *missio ad gentes*, directed toward that "mystery of unity," from which "it follows that all men and women who are saved share, though differently, in the same mystery of salvation in Jesus Christ through his Spirit."[5] Interreligious dialogue, which is part of the Church's evangelizing mission,[6] requires an attitude of understanding and a relationship of mutual knowledge and reciprocal enrichment, in obedience to the truth and with respect for freedom.[7]

3. In the practice of dialogue between the Christian faith and other religious traditions, as well as in seeking to understand its theoretical basis more deeply, new questions arise that need to be addressed through pursuing new paths of research, advancing proposals, and suggesting ways of acting that call for attentive discernment. In this task, the present Declaration seeks to recall to Bishops, theologians, and all the Catholic faithful, certain indispensable elements of Christian doctrine, which may help theological reflection in developing solutions consistent with the contents of the faith and responsive to the pressing needs of contemporary culture.

The expository language of the Declaration corresponds to its purpose, which is not to treat in a systematic manner the question of the unicity and salvific universality of the mystery of Jesus Christ and the Church, nor to propose solutions to questions that are matters of free theological debate, but rather to set forth again the doctrine of the Catholic faith in these areas, pointing out some fundamental questions that remain open to further development, and refuting specific positions that are erroneous or ambiguous. For this reason, the Declaration takes up what has been taught in previous Magisterial documents, in order to reiterate certain truths that are part of the Church's faith.

4. The Church's constant missionary proclamation is endangered today by relativistic theories which seek to justify religious pluralism, not only *de facto* but also *de iure* (or *in principle*). As a consequence, it is held that certain truths have been superseded; for example, the definitive and complete character of the revelation of Jesus Christ, the nature of Christian faith as compared with that of belief in other religions, the inspired nature of the books of Sacred Scripture, the personal unity between the Eternal Word and Jesus of Nazareth, the unity of the economy of the Incarnate Word and the Holy Spirit, the unicity and salvific universality of the mystery of Jesus Christ, the universal salvific mediation of the Church, the in-

separability — while recognizing the distinction — of the kingdom of God, the kingdom of Christ, and the Church, and the subsistence of the one Church of Christ in the Catholic Church.

The roots of these problems are to be found in certain presuppositions of both a philosophical and theological nature, which hinder the understanding and acceptance of the revealed truth. Some of these can be mentioned: the conviction of the elusiveness and inexpressibility of divine truth, even by Christian revelation; relativistic attitudes toward truth itself, according to which what is true for some would not be true for others; the radical opposition posited between the logical mentality of the West and the symbolic mentality of the East; the subjectivism which, by regarding reason as the only source of knowledge, becomes incapable of raising its "gaze to the heights, not daring to rise to the truth of being";[8] the difficulty in understanding and accepting the presence of definitive and eschatological events in history; the metaphysical emptying of the historical incarnation of the Eternal Logos, reduced to a mere appearing of God in history; the eclecticism of those who, in theological research, uncritically absorb ideas from a variety of philosophical and theological contexts without regard for consistency, systematic connection, or compatibility with Christian truth; finally, the tendency to read and to interpret Sacred Scripture outside the Tradition and Magisterium of the Church.

On the basis of such presuppositions, which may evince different nuances, certain theological proposals are developed — at times presented as assertions, and at times as hypotheses — in which Christian revelation and the mystery of Jesus Christ and the Church lose their character of absolute truth and salvific universality, or at least shadows of doubt and uncertainty are cast upon them.

I. The Fullness and Definitiveness of the Revelation of Jesus Christ

5. As a remedy for this relativistic mentality, which is becoming ever more common, it is necessary above all to reassert the definitive and complete character of the revelation of Jesus Christ. In fact, it must

be *firmly believed* that, in the mystery of Jesus Christ, the Incarnate Son of God, who is "the way, the truth, and the life" (Jn 14:6), the full revelation of divine truth is given: "No one knows the Son except the Father, and no one knows the Father except the Son and anyone to whom the Son wishes to reveal him" (Mt 11:27); "No one has ever seen God; God the only Son, who is in the bosom of the Father, has revealed him" (Jn 1:18); "For in Christ the whole fullness of divinity dwells in bodily form" (Col 2:9-10).

Faithful to God's word, the Second Vatican Council teaches: "By this revelation then, the deepest truth about God and the salvation of man shines forth in Christ, who is at the same time the mediator and the fullness of all revelation."[9] Furthermore, "Jesus Christ, therefore, the Word made flesh, sent 'as a man to men,' 'speaks the words of God' (Jn 3:34), and completes the work of salvation which his Father gave him to do (cf. Jn 5:36; 17:4). To see Jesus is to see his Father (cf. Jn 14:9). For this reason, Jesus perfected revelation by fulfilling it through his whole work of making himself present and manifesting himself: through his words and deeds, his signs and wonders, but especially through his death and glorious resurrection from the dead and finally with the sending of the Spirit of truth, he completed and perfected revelation and confirmed it with divine testimony. . . . The Christian dispensation, therefore, as the new and definitive covenant, will never pass away, and we now await no further new public revelation before the glorious manifestation of our Lord Jesus Christ (cf. 1 Tim 6:14 and Tit 2:13)."[10]

Thus, the Encyclical *Redemptoris Missio* calls the Church once again to the task of announcing the Gospel as the fullness of truth: "In this definitive Word of his revelation, God has made himself known in the fullest possible way. He has revealed to mankind who he is. This definitive self-revelation of God is the fundamental reason why the Church is missionary by her very nature. She cannot do other than proclaim the Gospel, that is, the fullness of the truth which God has enabled us to know about himself."[11] Only the revelation of Jesus Christ, therefore, "introduces into our history a universal and ultimate truth which stirs the human mind to ceaseless effort."[12]

6. Therefore, the theory of the limited, incomplete, or imperfect character of the revelation of Jesus Christ, which would be complementary to that found in other religions, is contrary to the Church's faith. Such a position would claim to be based on the notion that the truth about God cannot be grasped and manifested in its globality and completeness by any historical religion, neither by Christianity nor by Jesus Christ.

Such a position is in radical contradiction with the foregoing statements of Catholic faith according to which the full and complete revelation of the salvific mystery of God is given in Jesus Christ. Therefore, the words, deeds, and entire historical event of Jesus, though limited as human realities, have nevertheless the divine Person of the Incarnate Word, "true God and true man,"[13] as their subject. For this reason, they possess in themselves the definitiveness and completeness of the revelation of God's salvific ways, even if the depth of the divine mystery in itself remains transcendent and inexhaustible. The truth about God is not abolished or reduced because it is spoken in human language; rather, it is unique, full, and complete, because he who speaks and acts is the Incarnate Son of God. Thus, faith requires us to profess that the Word made flesh, in his entire mystery, who moves from incarnation to glorification, is the source, participated but real, as well as the fulfillment of every salvific revelation of God to humanity,[14] and that the Holy Spirit, who is Christ's Spirit, will teach this "entire truth" (Jn 16:13) to the Apostles and, through them, to the whole Church.

7. The proper response to God's revelation is *the obedience of faith* (Rom 16:26; cf. Rom 1:5; 2 Cor 10:5-6) by which man freely entrusts his entire self to God, offering 'the full submission of intellect and will to God who reveals' and freely assenting to the revelation given by him."[15] Faith is a gift of grace: "in order to have faith, the grace of God must come first and give assistance; there must also be the interior helps of the Holy Spirit, who moves the heart and converts it to God, who opens the eyes of the mind and gives 'to everyone joy and ease in assenting to and believing in the truth.' "[16]

The obedience of faith implies acceptance of the truth of Christ's revelation, guaranteed by God, who is Truth itself:[17] "Faith is first of all a personal adherence of man to God. At the same time, and inseparably, it is a *free assent to the whole truth that God has revealed*."[18] Faith, therefore, as "*a gift of God*" and as "*a supernatural virtue infused by him*,"[19] involves a dual adherence: to God who reveals and to the truth which he reveals, out of the trust which one has in him who speaks. Thus, "we must believe in no one but God: the Father, the Son and the Holy Spirit."[20]

For this reason, the distinction between *theological faith* and *belief* in the other religions must be *firmly held*. If faith is the acceptance in grace of revealed truth, which "makes it possible to penetrate the mystery in a way that allows us to understand it coherently,"[21] then belief, in the other religions, is that sum of experience and thought that constitutes the human treasury of wisdom and religious aspiration, which man in his search for truth has conceived and acted upon in his relationship to God and the Absolute.[22]

This distinction is not always borne in mind in current theological reflection. Thus, theological faith (the acceptance of the truth revealed by the One and Triune God) is often identified with belief in other religions, which is religious experience still in search of the absolute truth and still lacking assent to God who reveals himself. This is one of the reasons why the differences between Christianity and the other religions tend to be reduced at times to the point of disappearance.

8. The hypothesis of the inspired value of the sacred writings of other religions is also put forward. Certainly, it must be recognized that there are some elements in these texts which may be *de facto* instruments by which countless people throughout the centuries have been and still are able today to nourish and maintain their life-relationship with God. Thus, as noted above, the Second Vatican Council, in considering the customs, precepts, and teachings of the other religions, teaches that "although differing in many ways from her own teaching, these nevertheless often reflect a ray of that truth which enlightens all men."[23]

The Church's tradition, however, reserves the designation of *inspired texts* to the canonical books of the Old and New Testaments, since these are inspired by the Holy Spirit.[24] Taking up this tradition, the Dogmatic Constitution on Divine Revelation of the Second Vatican Council states: "For Holy Mother Church, relying on the faith of the apostolic age, accepts as sacred and canonical the books of the Old and New Testaments, whole and entire, with all their parts, on the grounds that, written under the inspiration of the Holy Spirit (cf. Jn 20:31; 2 Tim 3:16; 2 Pet 1:19-21; 3:15-16), they have God as their author, and have been handed on as such to the Church herself."[25] These books "firmly, faithfully, and without error, teach that truth which God, for the sake of our salvation, wished to see confided to the Sacred Scriptures."[26]

Nevertheless, God, who desires to call all peoples to himself in Christ and to communicate to them the fullness of his revelation and love, "does not fail to make himself present in many ways, not only to individuals, but also to entire peoples through their spiritual riches, of which their religions are the main and essential expression even when they contain 'gaps, insufficiencies and errors.' "[27] Therefore, the sacred books of other religions, which in actual fact direct and nourish the existence of their followers, receive from the mystery of Christ the elements of goodness and grace which they contain.

II. The Incarnate Logos and the Holy Spirit in the Work of Salvation

9. In contemporary theological reflection there often emerges an approach to Jesus of Nazareth that considers him a particular, finite, historical figure, who reveals the divine not in an exclusive way, but in a way complementary with other revelatory and salvific figures. The Infinite, the Absolute, the Ultimate Mystery of God would thus manifest itself to humanity in many ways and in many historical figures: Jesus of Nazareth would be one of these. More concretely, for some, Jesus would be one of the many faces which the Logos has assumed in the course of time to communicate with humanity in a salvific way.

Furthermore, to justify the universality of Christian salvation as well as the fact of religious pluralism, it has been proposed that there is an economy of the eternal Word that is valid also outside the Church and is unrelated to her, in addition to an economy of the incarnate Word. The first would have a greater universal value than the second, which is limited to Christians, though God's presence would be more full in the second.

10. These theses are in profound conflict with the Christian faith. The doctrine of faith must be *firmly believed* which proclaims that Jesus of Nazareth, son of Mary, and he alone, is the Son and the Word of the Father. The Word, which "was in the beginning with God" (Jn 1:2), is the same as he who "became flesh" (Jn 1:14). In Jesus, "the Christ, the Son of the living God" (Mt 16:16), "the whole fullness of divinity dwells in bodily form" (Col 2:9). He is the "only begotten Son of the Father, who is in the bosom of the Father" (Jn 1:18), his "beloved Son, in whom we have redemption. . . . In him the fullness of God was pleased to dwell, and through him, God was pleased to reconcile all things to himself, on earth and in the heavens, making peace by the blood of his Cross" (Col 1:13-14; 19-20).

Faithful to Sacred Scripture and refuting erroneous and reductive interpretations, the First Council of Nicaea solemnly defined its faith in: "Jesus Christ, the Son of God, the only begotten generated from the Father, that is, from the being of the Father, God from God, Light from Light, true God from true God, begotten, not made, one in being with the Father, through whom all things were made, those in heaven and those on earth. For us men and for our salvation, he came down and became incarnate, was made man, suffered, and rose again on the third day. He ascended to the heavens and shall come again to judge the living and the dead."[28] Following the teachings of the Fathers of the Church, the Council of Chalcedon also professed: "the one and the same Son, our Lord Jesus Christ, the same perfect in divinity and perfect in humanity, the same truly God and truly man . . ., one in being with the Father according to the divinity and one in being with us according to the humanity . . ., begotten of the Father before the ages according to the divinity and, in these last days, for us and our salvation, of Mary, the Virgin Mother of God, according to the humanity."[29]

For this reason, the Second Vatican Council states that Christ "the new Adam . . . 'image of the invisible God' (Col 1:15) is himself the perfect man who has restored that likeness to God in the children of Adam which had been disfigured since the first sin. . . . As an innocent lamb he merited life for us by his blood which he freely shed. In him God reconciled us to himself and to one another, freeing us from the bondage of the devil and of sin, so that each one of us could say with the apostle: the Son of God 'loved me and gave himself up for me' (Gal 2:20)."[30]

In this regard, John Paul II has explicitly declared: "To introduce any sort of separation between the Word and Jesus Christ is contrary to the Christian faith. . . . Jesus is the Incarnate Word — a single and indivisible person. . . . Christ is none other than Jesus of Nazareth; he is the Word of God made man for the salvation of all. . . . In the process of discovering and appreciating the manifold gifts — especially the spiritual treasures — that God has bestowed on every people, we cannot separate those gifts from Jesus Christ, who is at the center of God's plan of salvation."[31]

It is likewise contrary to the Catholic faith to introduce a separation between the salvific action of the Word as such and that of the Word made man. With the incarnation, all the salvific actions of the Word of God are always done in unity with the human nature that he has assumed for the salvation of all people. The one subject which operates in the two natures, human and divine, is the single person of the Word.[32]

Therefore, the theory which would attribute, after the incarnation as well, a salvific activity to the Logos as such in his divinity, exercised "in addition to" or "beyond" the humanity of Christ, is not compatible with the Catholic faith.[33]

11. Similarly, the doctrine of faith regarding the unicity of the salvific economy willed by the One and Triune God must be *firmly believed*, at the source and center of which is the mystery of the incarnation of the Word, mediator of divine grace on the level of creation

and redemption (cf. Col 1:15-20), he who recapitulates all things (cf. Eph 1:10), he "whom God has made our wisdom, our righteousness, and sanctification and redemption" (1 Cor 1:30). In fact, the mystery of Christ has its own intrinsic unity, which extends from the eternal choice in God to the parousia: "he [the Father] chose us in Christ before the foundation of the world to be holy and blameless before him in love" (Eph 1:4); "In Christ we are heirs, having been destined according to the purpose of him who accomplishes all things according to his counsel and will" (Eph 1:11); "For those whom he foreknew he also predestined to be conformed to the image of his Son, in order that he might be the firstborn among many brothers; those whom he predestined he also called; and those whom he called he also justified; and those whom he justified he also glorified" (Rom 8:29-30).

The Church's Magisterium, faithful to divine revelation, reasserts that Jesus Christ is the mediator and the universal redeemer: "The Word of God, through whom all things were made, was made flesh, so that as perfect man he could save all men and sum up all things in himself. The Lord . . . is he whom the Father raised from the dead, exalted and placed at his right hand, constituting him judge of the living and the dead."[34] This salvific mediation implies also the unicity of the redemptive sacrifice of Christ, eternal high priest (cf. Heb 6:20; 9:11; 10:12-14).

12. There are also those who propose the hypothesis of an economy of the Holy Spirit with a more universal breadth than that of the Incarnate Word, crucified and risen. This position also is contrary to the Catholic faith, which, on the contrary, considers the salvific incarnation of the Word as a trinitarian event. In the New Testament, the mystery of Jesus, the Incarnate Word, constitutes the place of the Holy Spirit's presence as well as the principle of the Spirit's effusion on humanity, not only in messianic times (cf. Acts 2:32-36; Jn 7:39; 20:22; 1 Cor 15:45), but also prior to his coming in history (cf. 1 Cor 10:4; 1 Pet 1:10-12).

The Second Vatican Council has recalled to the consciousness of the Church's faith this fundamental truth. In presenting the Father's salvific plan for all humanity, the Council closely links the mystery of Christ from its very beginnings with that of the Spirit.[35] The entire work of building the Church by Jesus Christ the Head, in the course of the centuries, is seen as an action which he does in communion with his Spirit.[36]

Furthermore, the salvific action of Jesus Christ, with and through his Spirit, extends beyond the visible boundaries of the Church to all humanity. Speaking of the paschal mystery, in which Christ even now associates the believer to himself in a living manner in the Spirit and gives him the hope of resurrection, the Council states: "All this holds true not only for Christians but also for all men of good will in whose hearts grace is active invisibly. For since Christ died for all, and since all men are in fact called to one and the same destiny, which is divine, we must hold that the Holy Spirit offers to all the possibility of being made partners, in a way known to God, in the paschal mystery."[37]

Hence, the connection is clear between the salvific mystery of the Incarnate Word and that of the Spirit, who actualizes the salvific efficacy of the Son made man in the lives of all people, called by God to a single goal, both those who historically preceded the Word made man and those who live after his coming in history: the Spirit of the Father, bestowed abundantly by the Son, is the animator of all (cf. Jn 3:34).

Thus, the recent Magisterium of the Church has firmly and clearly recalled the truth of a single divine economy: "The Spirit's presence and activity affect not only individuals but also society and history, peoples, cultures and religions. . . . The Risen Christ 'is now at work in human hearts through the strength of his Spirit.' . . . Again, it is the Spirit who sows the 'seeds of the word' present in various customs and cultures, preparing them for full maturity in Christ."[38] While recognizing the historical-salvific function of the Spirit in the whole universe and in the entire history of humanity,[39] the Magisterium states: "This is the same Spirit who was at work in the incarnation and in the life, death, and resurrection of Jesus and who is at work in the Church. He is therefore not an alternative to Christ nor does he fill a sort of void which is sometimes suggested as existing between Christ and the Logos.

Whatever the Spirit brings about in human hearts and in the history of peoples, in cultures and religions, serves as a preparation for the Gospel and can only be understood in reference to Christ, the Word who took flesh by the power of the Spirit 'so that as perfectly human he would save all human beings and sum up all things.' "[40]

In conclusion, the action of the Spirit is not outside or parallel to the action of Christ. There is only one salvific economy of the One and Triune God, realized in the mystery of the incarnation, death, and resurrection of the Son of God, actualized with the co-operation of the Holy Spirit, and extended in its salvific value to all humanity and to the entire universe: "No one, therefore, can enter into communion with God except through Christ, by the working of the Holy Spirit."[41]

III. Unicity and Universality of the Salvific Mystery of Jesus Christ

13. The thesis which denies the unicity and salvific universality of the mystery of Jesus Christ is also put forward. Such a position has no biblical foundation. In fact, the truth of Jesus Christ, Son of God, Lord and only Savior, who through the event of his incarnation, death and resurrection has brought the history of salvation to fulfill-ment, and which has in him its fullness and center, must be *firmly believed* as a constant element of the Church's faith.

The New Testament attests to this fact with clarity: "The Fa-ther has sent his Son as the Savior of the world" (1 Jn 4:14); "Behold the Lamb of God who takes away the sin of the world" (Jn 1:29). In his discourse before the Sanhedrin, Peter, in order to justify the heal-ing of a man who was crippled from birth, which was done in the name of Jesus (cf. Acts 3:1-8), proclaims: "There is salvation in no one else, for there is no other name under heaven given among men by which we must be saved" (Acts 4:12). St. Paul adds, moreover, that Jesus Christ "is Lord of all," "judge of the living and the dead," and thus "whoever believes in him receives forgiveness of sins through his name" (Acts 10:36, 42, 43).

Paul, addressing himself to the community of Corinth, writes: "Indeed, even though there may be so-called gods in heaven or on earth — as in fact there are many gods and many lords — yet for us there is one God, the Father, from whom are all things and for whom we exist, and one Lord, Jesus Christ, through whom are all things and through whom we exist" (1 Cor 8:5-6). Furthermore, John the Apostle states: "For God so loved the world that he gave his only Son, so that everyone who believes in him may not perish but may have eternal life. God did not send his Son into the world to condemn the world, but in order that the world might be saved through him" (Jn 3:16-17). In the New Testament, the universal salvific will of God is closely connected to the sole mediation of Christ: "[God] desires all men to be saved and to come to the knowledge of the truth. For there is one God; there is also one mediator between God and men, the man Jesus Christ, who gave himself as a ransom for all" (1 Tim 2:4-6).

It was in the awareness of the one universal gift of salvation offered by the Father through Jesus Christ in the Spirit (cf. Eph 1:3-14) that the first Christians encountered the Jewish people, showing them the fulfillment of salvation that went beyond the Law and, in the same awareness, they confronted the pagan world of their time, which aspired to salvation through a plurality of saviors. This inheritance of faith has been recalled recently by the Church's Magisterium: "The Church believes that Christ, who died and was raised for the sake of all (cf. 2 Cor 5:15) can, through his Spirit, give man the light and the strength to be able to respond to his highest calling, nor is there any other name under heaven given among men by which they can be saved (cf. Acts 4:12). The Church likewise believes that the key, the center, and the purpose of the whole of man's history is to be found in its Lord and Master."[42]

14. It must therefore be *firmly believed* as a truth of Catholic faith that the universal salvific will of the One and Triune God is offered and accomplished once for all in the mystery of the incarnation, death, and resurrection of the Son of God.

Bearing in mind this article of faith, theology today, in its reflection on the existence of other religious experiences and on their meaning in God's salvific plan, is invited to explore if and in what way the historical figures and positive elements of these religions may fall within the divine plan of salvation. In this undertaking, theological research has a vast field of work under the guidance of the Church's Magisterium. The Second Vatican Council, in fact, has stated that "the unique mediation of the Redeemer does not exclude, but rather gives rise to a manifold cooperation which is but a participation in this one source."[43] The content of this participated mediation should be explored more deeply, but must remain always consistent with the principle of Christ's unique mediation: "Although participated forms of mediation of different kinds and degrees are not excluded, they acquire meaning and value *only* from Christ's own mediation, and they cannot be understood as parallel or complementary to his."[44] Hence, those solutions that propose a salvific action of God beyond the unique mediation of Christ would be contrary to Christian and Catholic faith.

15. Not infrequently it is proposed that theology should avoid the use of terms like "unicity," "universality," and "absoluteness," which give the impression of excessive emphasis on the significance and value of the salvific event of Jesus Christ in relation to other religions. In reality, however, such language is simply being faithful to revelation, since it represents a development of the sources of the faith themselves. From the beginning, the community of believers has recognized in Jesus a salvific value such that he alone, as Son of God made man, crucified and risen, by the mission received from the Father and in the power of the Holy Spirit, bestows revelation (cf. Mt 11:27) and divine life (cf. Jn 1:12; 5:25-26; 17:2) to all humanity and to every person.

In this sense, one can and must say that Jesus Christ has a significance and a value for the human race and its history, which are unique and singular, proper to him alone, exclusive, universal, and absolute. Jesus is, in fact, the Word of God made man for the salvation of all. In expressing this consciousness of faith, the Second Vatican Council teaches: "The Word of God, through whom all things were made, was made flesh, so that as perfect man he could save all men and sum up all things in himself. The Lord is the goal of human history, the focal point of the desires of history and civilization, the center of mankind, the joy of all hearts, and the fulfillment of all aspirations. It is he whom the Father raised from the dead, exalted and placed at his right hand, constituting him judge of the living and the dead."[45] "It is precisely this uniqueness of Christ which gives him an absolute and universal significance whereby, while belonging to history, he remains history's center and goal: 'I am the Alpha and the Omega, the first and the last, the beginning and the end' (Rev 22:13)."[46]

IV. Unicity and Unity of the Church

16. The Lord Jesus, the only Savior, did not only establish a simple community of disciples, but constituted the Church as a *salvific mystery*: he himself is in the Church and the Church is in him (cf. Jn 15:1ff; Gal 3:28; Eph 4:15-16; Acts 9:5). Therefore, the fullness of Christ's salvific mystery belongs also to the Church, inseparably united to her Lord. Indeed, Jesus Christ continues his presence and his work of salvation in the Church and by means of the Church (cf. Col 1:24-27),[47] which is his body (cf. 1 Cor 12:12-13, 27; Col 1:18).[48] And thus, just as the head and members of a living body, though not identical, are inseparable, so too Christ and the Church can neither be confused nor separated, and constitute a single "whole Christ."[49] This same inseparability is also expressed in the New Testament by the analogy of the Church as the *Bride* of Christ (cf. 2 Cor 11:2; Eph 5:25-29; Rev 21:2, 9).[50]

Therefore, in connection with the unicity and universality of the salvific mediation of Jesus Christ, the unicity of the Church founded by him must be *firmly believed* as a truth of Catholic faith. Just as there is one Christ, so there exists a single body of Christ, a single Bride of Christ: "a single Catholic and apostolic Church."[51] Furthermore, the promises of the Lord that he would not abandon his Church (cf. Mt 16:18; 28:20) and that he would guide her by his Spirit (cf. Jn 16:13) mean, according to Catholic faith, that the unicity and the unity of the Church — like everything that belongs to the Church's integrity — will never be lacking.[52]

The Catholic faithful *are required to profess* that there is an historical continuity — rooted in the apostolic succession[53] — between the Church founded by Christ and the Catholic Church: "This is the single Church of Christ . . . which our Savior, after his resurrection, entrusted to Peter's pastoral care (cf. Jn 21:17), commissioning him and the other Apostles to extend and rule her (cf. Mt 28:18ff), erected for all ages as 'the pillar and mainstay of the truth' (1 Tim 3:15). This Church, constituted and organized as a society in the present world, subsists in [*subsistit in*] the Catholic Church, governed by the Successor of Peter and by the Bishops in communion with him."[54] With the expression *subsistit in*, the Second Vatican Council sought to harmonize two doctrinal statements: on the one hand, that the Church of Christ, despite the divisions which exist among Christians, continues to exist fully only in the Catholic Church, and on the other hand, that "outside of her structure, many elements can be found of sanctification and truth,"[55] that is, in those Churches and ecclesial communities which are not yet in full communion with the Catholic Church.[56] But with respect to these, it needs to be stated that "they derive their efficacy from the very fullness of grace and truth entrusted to the Catholic Church."[57]

17. Therefore, there exists a single Church of Christ, which subsists in the Catholic Church, governed by the Successor of Peter and by the Bishops in communion with him.[58] The Churches which, while not existing in perfect communion with the Catholic Church, remain united to her by means of the closest bonds, that is, by apostolic succession and a valid Eucharist, are true particular Churches.[59] Therefore, the Church of Christ is present and operative also in these Churches, even though they lack full communion with the Catholic Church, since they do not accept the Catholic doctrine of the Primacy, which, according to the will of God, the Bishop of Rome objectively has and exercises over the entire Church.[60]

On the other hand, the ecclesial communities which have not preserved the valid Episcopate and the genuine and integral substance of the Eucharistic mystery,[61] are not Churches in the proper sense; however, those who are baptized in these communities are, by Baptism, incorporated in Christ and thus are in a certain communion, albeit imperfect, with the Church.[62] Baptism in fact tends per se toward the full development of life in Christ, through the integral profession of faith, the Eucharist, and full communion in the Church.[63]

"The Christian faithful are therefore not permitted to imagine that the Church of Christ is nothing more than a collection — divided, yet in some way one — of Churches and ecclesial communities; nor are they free to hold that today the Church of Christ nowhere really exists, and must be considered only as a goal which all Churches and ecclesial communities must strive to reach."[64] In fact, "the elements of this already-given Church exist, joined together in their fullness in the Catholic Church and, without this fullness, in the other communities."[65] "Therefore, these separated Churches and communities as such, though we believe they suffer from defects, have by no means been deprived of significance and importance in the mystery of salvation. For the spirit of Christ has not refrained from using them as means of salvation which derive their efficacy from the very fullness of grace and truth entrusted to the Catholic Church."[66]

The lack of unity among Christians is certainly a *wound* for the Church; not in the sense that she is deprived of her unity, but "in that it hinders the complete fulfillment of her universality in history."[67]

V. The Church: Kingdom of God and Kingdom of Christ

18. The mission of the Church is "to proclaim and establish among all peoples the kingdom of Christ and of God, and she is on earth, the seed and the beginning of that kingdom."[68] On the one hand, the Church is "a sacrament — that is, sign and instrument of intimate union with God and of unity of the entire human race."[69] She is therefore the sign and instrument of the kingdom; she is called to announce and to establish the kingdom. On the other hand, the Church is the "people gathered by the unity of the Father, the Son and the Holy Spirit";[70] she is therefore "the kingdom of Christ al-

ready present in mystery"[71] and constitutes its *seed* and *beginning*. The kingdom of God, in fact, has an eschatological dimension: it is a reality present in time, but its full realization will arrive only with the completion or fulfillment of history.[72]

The meaning of the expressions *kingdom of heaven, kingdom of God,* and *kingdom of Christ* in Sacred Scripture and the Fathers of the Church, as well as in the documents of the Magisterium, is not always exactly the same, nor is their relationship to the Church, which is a mystery that cannot be totally contained by a human concept. Therefore, there can be various theological explanations of these terms. However, none of these possible explanations can deny or empty in any way the intimate connection between Christ, the kingdom, and the Church. In fact, the kingdom of God which we know from revelation, "cannot be detached either from Christ or from the Church. . . . If the kingdom is separated from Jesus, it is no longer the kingdom of God which he revealed. The result is a distortion of the meaning of the kingdom, which runs the risk of being transformed into a purely human or ideological goal and a distortion of the identity of Christ, who no longer appears as the Lord to whom everything must one day be subjected (cf. 1 Cor 15:27). Likewise, one may not separate the kingdom from the Church. It is true that the Church is not an end unto herself, since she is ordered toward the kingdom of God, of which she is the seed, sign and instrument. Yet, while remaining distinct from Christ and the kingdom, the Church is indissolubly united to both."[73]

19. To state the inseparable relationship between Christ and the kingdom is not to overlook the fact that the kingdom of God — even if considered in its historical phase — is not identified with the Church in her visible and social reality. In fact, "the action of Christ and the Spirit outside the Church's visible boundaries" must not be excluded.[74] Therefore, one must also bear in mind that "the kingdom is the concern of everyone: individuals, society and the world. Working for the kingdom means acknowledging and promoting God's activity, which is present in human history and transforms it. Building the kingdom means working for liberation from evil in all

its forms. In a word, the kingdom of God is the manifestation and the realization of God's plan of salvation in all its fullness."[75]

In considering the relationship between the kingdom of God, the kingdom of Christ, and the Church, it is necessary to avoid one-sided accentuations, as is the case with those "conceptions which deliberately emphasize the kingdom and which describe themselves as 'kingdom centered.' They stress the image of a Church which is not concerned about herself, but which is totally concerned with bearing witness to and serving the kingdom. It is a 'Church for others,' just as Christ is the 'man for others.' . . . Together with positive aspects, these conceptions often reveal negative aspects as well. First, they are silent about Christ: the kingdom of which they speak is 'theocentrically' based, since, according to them, Christ cannot be understood by those who lack Christian faith, whereas different peoples, cultures, and religions are capable of finding common ground in the one divine reality, by whatever name it is called. For the same reason, they put great stress on the mystery of creation, which is reflected in the diversity of cultures and beliefs, but they keep silent about the mystery of redemption. Furthermore, the kingdom, as they understand it, ends up either leaving very little room for the Church or undervaluing the Church in reaction to a presumed 'ecclesiocentrism' of the past and because they consider the Church herself only a sign, for that matter a sign not without ambiguity."[76] These theses are contrary to Catholic faith because they deny the unicity of the relationship which Christ and the Church have with the kingdom of God.

VI. The Church and the Other Religions in Relation to Salvation

20. From what has been stated above, some points follow that are necessary for theological reflection as it explores the relationship of the Church and the other religions to salvation.

Above all else, it must be *firmly believed* that "the Church, a pilgrim now on earth, is necessary for salvation: the one Christ is the mediator and the way of salvation; he is present to us in his body which is the Church. He himself explicitly asserted the necessity of faith and baptism (cf. Mk 16:16; Jn 3:5), and thereby affirmed at the same time the necessity of the Church which men enter through baptism as through a door."[77] This doctrine must not be set against the universal salvific will of God (cf. 1 Tim 2:4); "it is necessary to keep these two truths together, namely, the real possibility of salvation in Christ for all mankind and the necessity of the Church for this salvation."[78]

The Church is the "universal sacrament of salvation,"[79] since, united always in a mysterious way to the Savior Jesus Christ, her Head, and subordinated to him, she has, in God's plan, an indispensable relationship with the salvation of every human being.[80] For those who are not formally and visibly members of the Church, "salvation in Christ is accessible by virtue of a grace which, while having a mysterious relationship to the Church, does not make them formally part of the Church, but enlightens them in a way which is accommodated to their spiritual and material situation. This grace comes from Christ; it is the result of his sacrifice and is communicated by the Holy Spirit";[81] it has a relationship with the Church, which "according to the plan of the Father, has her origin in the mission of the Son and the Holy Spirit."[82]

21. With respect to the way in which the salvific grace of God — which is always given by means of Christ in the Spirit and has a mysterious relationship to the Church — comes to individual non-Christians, the Second Vatican Council limited itself to the statement that God bestows it "in ways known to himself."[83] Theologians are seeking to understand this question more fully. Their work is to be encouraged, since it is certainly useful for understanding better God's salvific plan and the ways in which it is accomplished. However, from what has been stated above about the mediation of Jesus Christ and the "unique and special relationship"[84] which the Church has with the kingdom of God among men — which in substance is the universal kingdom of Christ the Savior — it is clear that it would be contrary to the faith to consider the Church as one way of salvation alongside those constituted by the other religions, seen as complementary to the Church or substantially equivalent to her, even

if these are said to be converging with the Church toward the eschatological kingdom of God.

Certainly, the various religious traditions contain and offer religious elements which come from God,[85] and which are part of what "the Spirit brings about in human hearts and in the history of peoples, in cultures, and religions."[86] Indeed, some prayers and rituals of the other religions may assume a role of preparation for the Gospel, in that they are occasions or pedagogical helps in which the human heart is prompted to be open to the action of God.[87] One cannot attribute to these, however, a divine origin or an *ex opere operato* salvific efficacy, which is proper to the Christian sacraments.[88] Furthermore, it cannot be overlooked that other rituals, insofar as they depend on superstitions or other errors (cf. 1 Cor 10:20-21), constitute an obstacle to salvation.[89]

22. With the coming of the Savior Jesus Christ, God has willed that the Church founded by him be the instrument for the salvation of *all* humanity (cf. Acts 17:30-31).[90] This truth of faith does not lessen the sincere respect which the Church has for the religions of the world, but at the same time, it rules out, in a radical way, that mentality of indifferentism "characterized by a religious relativism which leads to the belief that 'one religion is as good as another.' "[91] If it is true that the followers of other religions can receive divine grace, it is also certain that *objectively speaking* they are in a gravely deficient situation in comparison with those who, in the Church, have the fullness of the means of salvation.[92] However, "all the children of the Church should nevertheless remember that their exalted condition results, not from their own merits, but from the grace of Christ. If they fail to respond in thought, word, and deed to that grace, not only shall they not be saved, but they shall be more severely judged."[93] One understands then that, following the Lord's command (cf. Mt 28:19-20) and as a requirement of her love for all people, the Church "proclaims and is in duty bound to proclaim without fail, Christ who is the way, the truth, and the life (Jn 14:6). In him, in whom God reconciled all things to himself (cf. 2 Cor 5:18-19), men find the fullness of their religious life."[94]

In interreligious dialogue as well, the mission *ad gentes* "today as always retains its full force and necessity."[95] "Indeed, God 'desires all men to be saved and come to the knowledge of the truth' (1 Tim 2:4); that is, God wills the salvation of everyone through the knowledge of the truth. Salvation is found in the truth. Those who obey the promptings of the Spirit of truth are already on the way of salvation. But the Church, to whom this truth has been entrusted, must go out to meet their desire, so as to bring them the truth. Because she believes in God's universal plan of salvation, the Church must be missionary."[96] Interreligious dialogue, therefore, as part of her evangelizing mission, is just one of the actions of the Church in her mission *ad gentes*.[97] *Equality*, which is a presupposition of interreligious dialogue, refers to the equal personal dignity of the parties in dialogue, not to doctrinal content, nor even less to the position of Jesus Christ — who is God himself made man — in relation to the founders of the other religions. Indeed, the Church, guided by charity and respect for freedom,[98] must be primarily committed to proclaiming to all people the truth definitively revealed by the Lord, and to announcing the necessity of conversion to Jesus Christ and of adherence to the Church through Baptism and the other sacraments, in order to participate fully in communion with God, the Father, Son and Holy Spirit. Thus, the certainty of the universal salvific will of God does not diminish, but rather increases the duty and urgency of the proclamation of salvation and of conversion to the Lord Jesus Christ.

Conclusion

23. The intention of the present *Declaration*, in reiterating and clarifying certain truths of the faith, has been to follow the example of the Apostle Paul, who wrote to the faithful of Corinth: "I handed on to you as of first importance what I myself received" (1 Cor 15:3). Faced with certain problematic and even erroneous propositions, theological reflection is called to reconfirm the Church's faith and to give reasons for her hope in a way that is convincing and effective.

In treating the question of the true religion, the Fathers of the Second Vatican Council taught: "We believe that this one true religion continues to exist in the Catholic and Apostolic Church, to which the Lord Jesus entrusted the task of spreading it among all people. Thus, he said to the Apostles: 'Go therefore and make disciples of all nations baptizing them in the name of the Father and of the Son and of the Holy Spirit, teaching them to observe all that I have commanded you' (Mt 28:19-20). Especially in those things that concern God and his Church, all persons are required to seek the truth, and when they come to know it, to embrace it and hold fast to it."[99]

The revelation of Christ will continue to be "the true lodestar"[100] in history for all humanity: "The truth, which is Christ, imposes itself as an all-embracing authority."[101] The Christian mystery, in fact, overcomes all barriers of time and space, and accomplishes the unity of the human family: "From their different locations and traditions all are called in Christ to share in the unity of the family of God's children. . . . Jesus destroys the walls of division and creates unity in a new and unsurpassed way through our sharing in his mystery. This unity is so deep that the Church can say with Saint Paul: 'You are no longer strangers and sojourners, but you are saints and members of the household of God' (Eph 2:19)."[102]

The Sovereign Pontiff John Paul II, at the Audience of June 16, 2000, granted to the undersigned Cardinal Prefect of the Congregation for the Doctrine of the Faith, with sure knowledge and by his apostolic authority, ratified and confirmed this Declaration, adopted in Plenary Session and ordered its publication.

Rome, from the Offices of the Congregation for the Doctrine of the Faith, August 6, 2000, the Feast of the Transfiguration of the Lord.

✠ Joseph Cardinal Ratzinger
Prefect

✠ Tarcisio Bertone, S.D.B.
Archbishop Emeritus of Vercelli
Secretary

Notes

1. First Council of Constantinople, *Symbolum Constantinopolitanum*: DS 150.

2. Cf. John Paul II, Encyclical Letter *Redemptoris Missio*, 1: *AAS* 83 (1991), 249-340.

3. Cf. Second Vatican Council, Decree *Ad Gentes* and Declaration *Nostra Aetate*; cf. also Paul VI, Apostolic Exhortation *Evangelii Nuntiandi*: *AAS* 68 (1976), 5-76; John Paul II, Encyclical Letter *Redemptoris Missio*.

4. Second Vatican Council, Declaration *Nostra Aetate*, 2.

5. Pontifical Council for Interreligious Dialogue and the Congregation for the Evangelization of Peoples, Instruction *Dialogue and Proclamation*, 29: *AAS* 84 (1992), 424; cf. Second Vatican Council, Pastoral Constitution *Gaudium et Spes*, 22.

6. Cf. John Paul II, Encyclical Letter *Redemptoris Missio*, 55: *AAS* 83 (1991), 302-304.

7. Cf. Pontifical Council for Interreligious Dialogue and the Congregation for the Evangelization of Peoples, Instruction *Dialogue and Proclamation*, 9: *AAS* 84 (1992), 417ff.

8. John Paul II, Encyclical Letter *Fides et Ratio*, 5: *AAS* 91 (1999), 5-88.

9. Second Vatican Council, Dogmatic Constitution *Dei Verbum*, 2.

10. *Ibid.*, 4.

11. John Paul II, Encyclical Letter *Redemptoris Missio*, 5.

12. John Paul II, Encyclical Letter *Fides et Ratio*, 14.

13. Council of Chalcedon, *Symbolum Chalcedonense*: DS 301; cf. St. Athanasius, *De Incarnatione*, 54, 3: *SC* 199, 458.

14. Second Vatican Council, Dogmatic Constitution *Dei Verbum*, 4.

15. *Ibid.*, 5.

16. *Ibid.*

17. Cf. *Catechism of the Catholic Church*, 144.

18. *Ibid.*, 150.

19. *Ibid.*, 153.

20. *Ibid.*, 178.

21. John Paul II, Encyclical Letter *Fides et Ratio*, 13.

22. Cf. *ibid.*, 31-32.

23. Second Vatican Council, Declaration *Nostra Aetate*, 2; cf. Second Vatican Council, Decree *Ad Gentes*, 9, where it speaks of the elements of good present "in the particular customs and cultures of peoples"; Dogmatic Constitution *Lumen Gentium*, 16, where it mentions the elements

of good and of truth present among non-Christians, which can be considered a preparation for the reception of the Gospel.

24. Cf. Council of Trent, *Decretum de libris sacris et de traditionibus recipiendis*: DS 1501; First Vatican Council, Dogmatic Constitution *Dei Filius*, cap. 2: DS 3006.

25. Second Vatican Council, Dogmatic Constitution *Dei Verbum*, 11.

26. *Ibid.*

27. John Paul II, Encyclical Letter *Redemptoris Missio*, 55; cf. 56 and Paul VI, Apostolic Exhortation *Evangelii Nuntiandi*, 53.

28. First Council of Nicaea, *Symbolum Nicaenum*: DS 125.

29. Council of Chalcedon, *Symbolum Chalcedonense*: DS 301.

30. Second Vatican Council, Pastoral Constitution *Gaudium et Spes*, 22.

31. John Paul II, Encyclical Letter *Redemptoris Missio*, 6.

32. Cf. St. Leo the Great, *Tomus ad Flavianum*: DS 294.

33. Cf. St. Leo the Great, Letter to the Emperor Leo I *Promisisse me memini*: DS 318: "... *in tantam unitatem ab ipso conceptu Virginis deitate et humanitate conserta, ut nec sine homine divina, nec sine Deo agerentur humana.*" Cf. also *ibid.* DS 317.

34. Second Vatican Council, Pastoral Constitution *Gaudium et Spes*, 45; cf. also Council of Trent, *Decretum de peccato originali*, 3: DS 1513.

35. Cf. Second Vatican Council, Dogmatic Constitution *Lumen Gentium*, 3-4.

36. Cf. *ibid.*, 7; cf. St. Irenaeus, who wrote that it is in the Church "that communion with Christ has been deposited, that is to say: the Holy Spirit" (*Adversus haereses* III, 24, 1: *SC* 211, 472).

37. Second Vatican Council, Pastoral Constitution *Gaudium et Spes*, 22.

38. John Paul II, Encyclical Letter *Redemptoris Missio*, 28. For the "seeds of the Word" cf. also St. Justin Martyr, *Second Apology* 8, 1-2; 10, 1-3; 13, 3-6: ed. E.J. Goodspeed, 84; 85; 88-89.

39. Cf. John Paul II, Encyclical Letter *Redemptoris Missio*, 28-29.

40. *Ibid.*, 29.

41. *Ibid.*, 5.

42. Second Vatican Council, Pastoral Constitution *Gaudium et Spes*, 10. Cf. St. Augustine, who wrote that Christ is the way, which "has never been lacking to mankind ... and apart from this way no one has been set free, no one is being set free, no one will be set free" (*De Civitate Dei* 10, 32, 2: *CCSL* 47, 312).

43. Second Vatican Council, Dogmatic Constitution *Lumen Gentium*, 62.

44. John Paul II, Encyclical Letter *Redemptoris Missio*, 5.

45. Second Vatican Council, Pastoral Constitution *Gaudium et Spes*, 45. The necessary and absolute singularity of Christ in human history is well expressed by St. Irenaeus in contemplating the preeminence of Jesus as firstborn Son: "In the heavens, as firstborn of the Father's counsel, the perfect Word governs and legislates all things; on the earth, as firstborn of the Virgin, a man just and holy, reverencing God and pleasing to God, good and perfect in every way, he saves from hell all those who follow him since he is the firstborn from the dead and Author of the life of God" (*Demonstratio apostolica*, 39: *SC* 406, 138).

46. John Paul II, Encyclical Letter *Redemptoris Missio*, 6.

47. Cf. Second Vatican Council, Dogmatic Constitution *Lumen Gentium*, 14.

48. Cf. *ibid.*, 7.

49. Cf. St. Augustine, *Enarratio in Psalmos*, Ps. 90, *Sermo* 2,1: *CCSL* 39, 1266; St. Gregory the Great, *Moralia in Iob*, Praefatio, 6, 14: PL 75, 525; St. Thomas Aquinas, *Summa Theologiae*, III, q. 48, a. 2 ad 1.

50. Cf. Second Vatican Council, Dogmatic Constitution *Lumen Gentium*, 6.

51. *Symbolum maius Ecclesiae Armeniacae*: DS 48. Cf. Boniface VIII, *Unam sanctam*: DS 870-872; Second Vatican Council, Dogmatic Constitution *Lumen Gentium*, 8.

52. Cf. Second Vatican Council, Decree *Unitatis Redintegratio*, 4; John Paul II, Encyclical Letter *Ut Unum Sint*, 11: *AAS* 87 (1995), 927.

53. Cf. Second Vatican Council, Dogmatic Constitution *Lumen Gentium*, 20; cf. also St. Irenaeus, *Adversus haereses*, III, 3, 1-3: *SC* 211, 20-44; St. Cyprian, *Epist.* 33, 1: *CCSL* 3B, 164-165; St. Augustine, *Contra adver. legis et prophet.*, 1, 20, 39: *CCSL* 49, 70.

54. Second Vatican Council, Dogmatic Constitution *Lumen Gentium*, 8.

55. Ibid.; cf. John Paul II, Encyclical Letter *Ut Unum Sint*, 13. Cf. also Second Vatican Council, Dogmatic Constitution *Lumen Gentium*, 15 and the Decree *Unitatis Redintegratio*, 3.

56. The interpretation of those who would derive from the formula *subsistit in* the thesis that the one Church of Christ could subsist also in non-Catholic Churches and ecclesial communities is therefore contrary to the authentic meaning of *Lumen Gentium*. "The Council instead chose the word *subsistit* precisely to clarify that there exists only one 'subsis-

tence' of the true Church, while outside her visible structure there only exist *elementa Ecclesiae*, which — being elements of that same Church — tend and lead toward the Catholic Church" (Congregation for the Doctrine of the Faith, *Notification on the Book "Church: Charism and Power" by Father Leonardo Boff: AAS* 77 [1985], 756-762).

57. Second Vatican Council, Decree *Unitatis Redintegratio*, 3.

58. Cf. Congregation for the Doctrine of the Faith, Declaration *Mysterium Ecclesiae*, 1: *AAS* 65 (1973), 396-398.

59. Cf. Second Vatican Council, Decree *Unitatis Redintegratio*, 14 and 15; Congregation for the Doctrine of the Faith, Letter *Communionis notio*, 17: *AAS* 85 (1993), 848.

60. Cf. First Vatican Council, Constitution *Pastor Aeternus*: DS 3053-3064; Second Vatican Council, Dogmatic Constitution *Lumen Gentium*, 22.

61. Cf. Second Vatican Council, Decree *Unitatis Redintegratio*, 22.

62. Cf. *ibid.*, 3.

63. Cf. *ibid.*, 22.

64. Congregation for the Doctrine of the Faith, Declaration *Mysterium Ecclesiae*, 1.

65. John Paul II, Encyclical Letter *Ut Unum Sint*, 14.

66. Second Vatican Council, Decree *Unitatis Redintegratio*, 3.

67. Congregation for the Doctrine of the Faith, Letter *Communionis notio*, 17; cf. Second Vatican Council, Decree *Unitatis Redintegratio*, 4.

68. Second Vatican Council, Dogmatic Constitution *Lumen Gentium*, 5.

69. *Ibid.*, 1.

70. *Ibid.*, 4. Cf. St. Cyprian, *De Dominica oratione* 23: *CCSL* 3A, 105.

71. Second Vatican Council, Dogmatic Constitution *Lumen Gentium*, 3.

72. Cf. *ibid.*, 9; cf. also the prayer addressed to God found in the *Didache* 9, 4: *SC* 248, 176: "May the Church be gathered from the ends of the earth into your kingdom" and *ibid.* 10, 5: *SC* 248, 180: "Remember, Lord, your Church . . . and, made holy, gather her together from the four winds into your kingdom which you have prepared for her."

73. John Paul II, Encyclical Letter *Redemptoris Missio*, 18; cf. Apostolic Exhortation *Ecclesia in Asia*, 17: *L'Osservatore Romano* (Nov. 7, 1999). The kingdom is so inseparable from Christ that, in a certain sense, it is identified with him (cf. Origen, *In Mt. Hom.*, 14, 7: *PG* 13, 1197; Tertullian, *Adversus Marcionem*, IV, 33,8: *CCSL* 1, 634).

74. John Paul II, Encyclical Letter *Redemptoris Missio*, 18.

75. *Ibid.*, 15.

76. *Ibid.*, 17.

77. Second Vatican Council, Dogmatic Constitution *Lumen Gentium*, 14; cf. Decree *Ad Gentes*, 7; Decree *Unitatis Redintegratio*, 3.

78. John Paul II, Encyclical Letter *Redemptoris Missio*, 9; cf. *Catechism of the Catholic Church*, 846-847.

79. Second Vatican Council, Dogmatic Constitution *Lumen Gentium*, 48.

80. Cf. St. Cyprian, *De catholicae ecclesiae unitate*, 6: *CCSL* 3, 253-254; St. Irenaeus, *Adversus haereses*, III, 24, 1: *SC* 211, 472-474.

81. John Paul II, Encyclical Letter *Redemptoris Missio*, 10.

82. Second Vatican Council, Decree *Ad Gentes*, 2. The famous formula *extra Ecclesiam nullus omnino salvatur* is to be interpreted in this sense (cf. Fourth Lateran Council, Cap. 1. *De fide catholica*: DS 802). Cf. also the *Letter of the Holy Office to the Archbishop of Boston*: DS 3866-3872.

83. Second Vatican Council, Decree *Ad Gentes*, 7.

84. John Paul II, Encyclical Letter *Redemptoris Missio*, 18.

85. These are the seeds of the divine Word (*semina Verbi*), which the Church recognizes with joy and respect (cf. Second Vatican Council, Decree *Ad Gentes*, 11; Declaration *Nostra Aetate*, 2).

86. John Paul II, Encyclical Letter *Redemptoris Missio*, 29.

87. Cf. *ibid.*; *Catechism of the Catholic Church*, 843.

88. Cf. Council of Trent, *Decretum de sacramentis*, can. 8, *de sacramentis in genere*: DS 1608.

89. Cf. John Paul II, Encyclical Letter *Redemptoris Missio*, 55.

90. Cf. Second Vatican Council, Dogmatic Constitution *Lumen Gentium*, 17; John Paul II, Encyclical Letter *Redemptoris Missio*, 11.

91. John Paul II, Encyclical Letter *Redemptoris Missio*, 36.

92. Cf. Pius XII, Encyclical Letter *Mystici Corporis*: DS 3821.

93. Second Vatican Council, Dogmatic Constitution *Lumen Gentium*, 14.

94. Second Vatican Council, Declaration *Nostra Aetate*, 2.

95. Second Vatican Council, Decree *Ad Gentes*, 7.

96. *Catechism of the Catholic Church*, 851; cf. also 849-856.

97. Cf. John Paul II, Encyclical Letter *Redemptoris Missio*, 55; Apostolic Exhortation *Ecclesia in Asia*, 31.

98. Cf. Second Vatican Council, Declaration *Dignitatis Humanae*, 1.

99. *Ibid.*

100. John Paul II, Encyclical Letter *Fides et Ratio*, 15.

101. *Ibid.*, 92.

102. *Ibid.*, 70.

ABOUT THE AUTHOR

REV. PETER M.J. STRAVINSKAS, Ph.D., S.T.D., is one of the Church's most accomplished and prolific authors. The editor of the popular apologetics magazine *The Catholic Answer*, he is the author or editor of numerous books including *Our Sunday Visitor's Catholic Dictionary, Revised*; *Our Sunday Visitor's Catholic Encyclopedia, Revised Edition*; and *The Catholic Response, Revised and Updated*.

NOTES

NOTES

NOTES

NOTES

NOTES

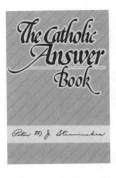

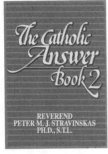

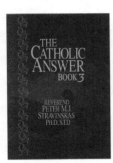

FATHER PETER STRAVINSKAS HAS *THE CATHOLIC ANSWER* FOR YOU!

Since 1987, inquiring Catholic minds have turned to Our Sunday Visitor's bimonthly magazine *The Catholic Answer*, edited by Father Stravinskas, for the answers to such questions as:

- Can anyone other than a Catholic ever receive Holy Communion in a Catholic Church? (Book 1)
- If a Catholic still has guilty feelings about past sins, what should he do? (Book 2)
- Why did the Lord God give Satan the power to do with Job as he willed? (Book 3)

Now you, too, can discover the solid Catholic answers to these and many other questions gleaned from the pages of this award-winning magazine and compiled in a handy book format.

The Catholic Answer Book, 0-87973-458-2, **(458)** paper, 192 pp.

The Catholic Answer Book 2, 0-87973-737-9, **(737)** paper, 240 pp.

The Catholic Answer Book 3, 0-87973-933-9, **(933)** paper, 304 pp.

OurSundayVisitor

200 Noll Plaza, Huntington, IN 46750
Toll Free: **1-800-348-2440**
E-mail: osvbooks@osv.com
Website: www.osv.com

Availability of products subject to change without notice.   A29BBABP

A Resource for the Church
of the Twenty-first Century

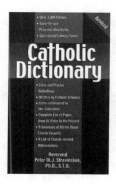

- **MORE THAN 3,000 ENTRIES:** There are thousands of listings for topics covering theology, doctrine, canon law, saints, liturgy, vestments, architecture, religious orders, holy days, and catechetics. A collaborative effort by Catholic scholars, this work was compiled and edited by Father Peter M.J. Stravinskas.

- **CONCISE DEFINITIONS:** Each entry provides all essential information as well as an easy-to-use pronunciation guide. The entries are cross-referenced to the *Catechism of the Catholic Church.*

- **SPECIALIZED CATHOLIC LISTS:** A list of all the popes is included, along with the councils of the Church and their chief doctrines.

Order your copy today!
Catholic Dictionary, Revised, 0-87973-390-X, (390) paper, 800 pp.

Our Sunday Visitor

200 Noll Plaza, Huntington, IN 46750
Toll Free: **1-800-348-2440**
E-mail: osvbooks@osv.com
Website: www.osv.com

Availability of products subject to change without notice.   A29BBABP

Our Sunday Visitor . . .
Your Source for Discovering the Riches of the Catholic Faith

Our Sunday Visitor has an extensive line of materials for young children, teens, and adults. Our books, Bibles, booklets, CD-ROMs, audios, and videos are available in bookstores worldwide.

To receive a FREE full-line catalog or for more information, call **Our Sunday Visitor** at **1-800-348-2440**. Or write, **Our Sunday Visitor** / 200 Noll Plaza / Huntington, IN 46750.

- -

Please send me: __A catalog
Please send me materials on:
__Apologetics and catechetics   __Reference works
__Prayer books   __Heritage and the saints
__The family   __The parish
Name_____
Address_____Apt._____
City_____State_____Zip_____
Telephone (   ) _____

A29BBABP

- -

Please send a friend: __A catalog
Please send a friend materials on:
__Apologetics and catechetics   __Reference works
__Prayer books   __Heritage and the saints
__The family   __The parish
Name_____
Address_____Apt._____
City_____State_____Zip_____
Telephone (   ) _____

A29BBABP

- -

OurSundayVisitor
——

200 Noll Plaza, Huntington, IN 46750
Toll Free: **1-800-348-2440**
E-mail: osvbooks@osv.com
Website: www.osv.com